THAT'S MY PROPERTY

How Purpose Turned a Chicago Gang Member Into an Apartment Investor & How You Can Become One Too

SECOND EDITION

DRE EVANS

To:

From:

Praise for That's My Property

"As a newcomer into the real estate business, I was looking for something that not only taught me but inspired me. I have read many books on real estate, but "That's My Property" taught me more about multifamily and syndications than any other. I feel confident and inspired by Dre Evans' words in this book. I am able to jump head first into the business without hesitations! Dre's life story, a gang member from the south side of Chicago to a successful real estate investor, proves there are truly no excuses! His realness and rawness in the book make me feel as if he is speaking to me directly! I know if he can do it, I can too, especially with the guidance and clarity he has provided me. Patiently waiting on more books from him."

- ANDREEA NATALIA
CEO, Kaffeology Cafe & Coffee Shops

"For someone who is still learning the power and impact of investing while building personal wealth, this motivating and inspiring book takes a venture into the real estate lane, providing many different examples and ways to successfully do so. The author Dre Evans gives many testaments on how his own life transforms from inner-city Chicago, becoming a proud Naval Academy graduate, to a prosperous real estate investor. If you want to expand your level of knowledge and receive the value and benefits that come with property investing, I highly recommend reading this book! You will be far from disappointed and be able to share this information with others."

- FREDDY SIMPSON
Naval Academy Graduate & Investor

"That's My Property" is beyond impressive and inspiring, it is so much more than just another "how-to book." Evans' riveting personal stories on what led him to real estate investing and how it has transformed his life was so compelling it made me not want to put it down! The author is obviously well versed in multifamily real estate investment and breaks down every step of the process in a clear and easy-to-understand way so even someone like me, who is new to this business, feels like I know how to get started. The book is packed full of knowledge and insider information by someone who clearly has had a great deal of success in this business. Definitely a great read and worthwhile investment for your future. I highly recommend."

- CRAIG BANDES
CEO, Pixelligent Technologies

"Dre does an amazing job in this book sharing his personal story and his transition to becoming a real estate investor. He lays out a simple-to-follow guide to help you get into the "game" yourself and does an excellent job explaining everything in detail. I would highly recommend this book."

- JESSE DILILLO
CEO, JSJ Investments & Active Syndicator

"Real and raw book. Realtors and investors need to read a book as valuable as this. Dre shares his testimony and it's very VERY inspiring. One of my favorite lines in the book was "Be different - and be proud of it." I've always felt different and this line alone was enough to get me fired up about investing and changing my life for the better. Can't wait to read the next book! Thanks Dre!!"

- JASMINE WILLIAMS
Real Estate Agent, Acropolis Developments

"Dre Evans story inspires readers that no matter what your background is you CAN become successful in real estate investing. Having known Dre for a while, it was no surprise to me how well-written this book is as he is an all-or-nothing kind of individual. Highly recommend you pick up a copy and start your investing journey today."

- JONATHAN NICHOLS
CEO, Apogee Capital & Multifamily Investor

"What an absolute breath of fresh air reading this book! That's My Property allowed me to sit back and recall moments when I felt times were tough during a real estate transaction. Dre Evans provided great knowledge for someone who is ready for the next big step in their investment life. Recommend 1000%!!"

- PABLO ROMERO
Feleez Estate LLC, a Real Estate Investment Firm

"Andre opens up and tells his remarkable story of struggle and success and provides an incredible amount of educational tips along the way. It's a must-read!"

- CLIFF LUBER
CEO, Upward Capital & Active Syndicator

"Dre does a good job recapping his tough childhood and how that inspired him to take control of his future, focusing on the mindsets needed to be successful. His path to venture into and succeed in real estate is inspirational, and this book does a good job introducing key concepts to multifamily real estate - all while helping the reader form a plan along the way!"

- COREY SCHNEIDER
Multifamily Real Estate Investor

"Very Informative for newcomers into multifamily investing. Dre's life story helps paint the picture of how multifamily investing can change one's life. He gives hope to people who are looking to better themselves and their families. I enjoyed how he simplified certain real estate terms to better understand how they apply to investing in real estate. I've read this book twice already and I'm pretty sure I'll be reading it a few more times."

- NICHOLAS BERRIOS
Veteran & Real Estate Investor

"Great amount of value in this book and Dre's journey is truly inspiring."

- Zed Truong
Real Estate Investor

"The personalization and realness in the words makes you appreciate where this book comes from. Dre, you did an amazing job, congrats!!"
- Maxine
Real Estate Investor

Dedication

For my mother: my WHY in life.

To all those out there fighting the fight, working hard and searching for a way to achieve passive income and the freedom of time.

To kids in Chicago who struggle to dream and fight to survive the vicious grip of the streets.

To all my That's My Property investors and the Multifamily By the Slice Podcast listeners.

This is for you.

Contents

HOW TO USE THIS BOOK

How many opportunities have you missed out on because you failed to act on and apply the knowledge you have read? Too many to count, probably, right? You are reading this book because there is something inside of you that craves more from life through passive income and the freedom of time—and you know real estate is the best way to get you there.

When I graduated from the U.S. Naval Academy, I gained a deep-seated discipline for how people use their time effectively. When I teach and educate, my focus is on inspiring people to actually ACT and achieve RESULTS. This is a quality demanded from you as a Naval Officer.

You are expected to lead sailors and marines in danger and to value their time. Every task I give them, every word I utter out of my mouth, must *count.* And ultimately, it must propel them to *act* in a meaningful way or to accomplish a certain task.

This book is no different.

I will not waste your time.

And you will act and *do something* at the end of this book. At a minimum, you must do these three things:

1. Prepare to reset your mind on what you think you know about money and investing. Write down your goals for life and real estate in a journal, on a napkin, a dry erase board, or a sheet of paper. Hell, I don't care what you write them down on—JUST

WRITE THEM DOWN. To help assist you, I have provided multiple goal planners at the back of this book.

2. Take notes on whatever questions you have, then reach out and ask me about them. I'm an open book and will help in any way I can.
3. TAKE ONE STEP: Decide to step out of fear and actually invest in multifamily real estate to achieve legacy wealth. If you don't do it for yourself, do it for your family or those you love. Or do it for the youth and people you will inspire.

Thank you for purchasing this book. I know you could have picked any number of books to read, but you picked this book and for that, I am grateful.

If you enjoyed this book and found value from reading it, I'd like to hear from you and hope you could take some time to leave a review on Amazon.

Your feedback and support help impact the lives of other readers to find the right book for their needs.

I wish you all the best in your future success!

SCAN TO LEAVE A REVIEW ON AMAZON

INTRODUCTION

"To create real change in your life, you need to shed your current actions and thoughts that aren't serving your long-term and short-term goals. To live a bigger life, you need to learn how to be a bigger human being."
– Matt Faircloth

Welcome, motivators! The first step in true change is acknowledgment. I salute you for following that burning desire within your heart to expand your knowledge about multifamily real estate, in addition to becoming a better person that will add value to this world.

That's My Property is a blueprint for those of you who want to learn how to get started in investing in apartment real estate.

This book will teach you how to be fearless and to obtain the power that comes from positive affirmations and written goals. Most importantly, you are reading an amazing tool that will challenge you to become a better version of yourself.

This book is divided into three main parts. In the first section, The Beginning, I walk readers through a glimpse of what life was like for me growing up on the South Side of Chicago as a former gang member.

In Section 2, The Journey: My First Multifamily Deal, I will explain step-by-step how I bought my first apartment building in San Diego, California and the struggles and lessons I learned along the way. You will have a front-row seat into my thought process and emotions. I will explain what it takes to succeed as a real estate investor and how it can be a powerful tool for financial independence.

Finally, in Section 3, Our Journey: Multifamily Real Estate Education, we will dig deep into the trenches of learning about the basics of apartment investing, key terminology, and the ins and outs of multifamily syndications.

Throughout the book, you will notice I have also included multiple bonus material checklists, graphics, and outlines, to help aid in your education process and make investing easier for you. When you come across a QR code within the text, simply scan it using your smartphone camera to access these valuable resources.

This is an easy-to-use book. It is designed so that you can read the entire text in order or jump to the particular chapter topic that you would like to learn about.

In these pages, you will hear personal stories you can relate to. You'll see that at heart, I'm just a kid from Chicago. I was not born into wealth. I wasn't given a handout. The odds and stereotypes were stacked against me. Yet, I overcame and became successful in real estate, and I'm driven to accomplish much more.

You can do this too.

All it takes is the right mindset, education, and a purposeful heart.

Congratulations again on having the courage to become a better version of yourself for your family, friends, and those you will inspire (whom you haven't even met yet).

Now lace your boot straps up tight—and let's get into it!

PART I

THE BEGINNING

Chapter 1

YOU GOTTA HAVE HEART

Life happens quickly, and any choice you make can be your last. I learned this early as a child on the playgrounds at school, on the sidewalks, and on the street corners. On the South Side of Chicago, I was like most: a skinny kid up against the brawling bullies and fighting to survive to live another day. One out of a triplet, my brothers and I all tried to follow in the footsteps of our beloved mother, with grace and trust in God. That wasn't enough to save us from the violence that was there from the moment we stepped foot out the door to the moment we were home safe and sound. Every step was like walking around in a jungle, never knowing who would be doing the harassing that day. Either way, the odds were stacked against us. There were so many shootings and underage killings. Kids took the risk and walked in the middle of the street with cars to avoid the stray bullets. It was common for kids in our neighborhood to pray to God they'd make it to twenty-one.

I grew up in a war zone. And that war eventually transferred itself to my heart and compelled me to join the streets.

"Sometimes you have to pick the gun up to put the gun down."
– Malcom X

I remember when I beat this guy's jaw in with a gun.

And at the time, I enjoyed it. Most people call this pistol-whipping. This is how it went down that day: It was gloomy in Chicago, which is known for its bipolar weather. I was fourteen, meeting up with a group of guys who were also members of the gang. We met in a parking lot. We were just chilling and shooting the breeze. Then we saw this guy—who was affiliated with another gang—walking past us across the street. He appeared to be alone.

My friend Jake said, "Yo, Dre, that's that dude that was talking crap and threatened to go after your brothers. You should go over there and show him what's up. Go handle your business, bro."

At this, Jake slid a pistol into my hands. I loved the feeling of the steel. It made me feel powerful and unstoppable. I remember how warm it was from being pressed against his skin within the waistband of his sagging pants. I quickly grabbed the gun and stuffed it behind the back of my waistline, covering it up with my long Academics brand T-shirt.

I knew this guy, the enemy, would notice me walking over and immediately be on guard. Like a chameleon, I changed up my entire body language and demeanor. I gave him a friendly wave and a slight smile as I approached him. Halfway across the street, I said something to myself along the lines of, "I'm gonna be fine. I'll mess this dude up and walk away scratch-free. You got this, Dre."

Even before I knew what I was doing, I was applying the power of affirmation into manifestation, even if it was in the name of a quarrel, machismo, and ultimate street credibility. Little did I also know these key qualities would allow me to become a successful real estate investor years later.

Back to the action: mano a mano, man to man—he already knew who I was and who I was affiliated with, so I had to be careful. When he first noticed me jogging across the street, I saw his face harden, and his whole body plump up in a defensive stance. I remember seeing his hand move toward his waistline to grip and draw his gun for protection. "It's all good, yo," I said and lifted my hands up. "I just wanna talk." When I finally reached his face, I threw him a handshake to throw him off guard. Just as he reached his hand out to mine, I grabbed his arm, pulled him toward me with one hard jerk, and gave him a solid right hook to the face.

Animal survivalism took over, and what I saw next was mostly RED. I took the gun tucked in the back of my sagging pants and proceeded to beat him viciously with it. It was so visceral; dreamlike in many ways. It was fall in Chicago, and as if out of character, I watched the autumn leaves splatter with his blood.

In the gang, we had values. As a man, I have values. I knew that if I didn't set the tone for how I wanted to be perceived and what I would tolerate from others—I would forever be perceived as a target or as weak. This guy threatened my brothers and family, so it had to be addressed. I didn't kill him, but he left that day with a black and blue face covered in red and a broken jaw.

I used to take pride in being tough. I took pride in the fights. I took pride every time I wielded a gun in my hand and pulled the trigger (despite it being wrong).

Today, I have transferred that raw pride into an ethical pride in working in real estate and being a provider of opportunities. The Naval Academy sharpened my values as a man and as a leader. In multifamily real estate, I've set the tone and clarified how I want to be perceived as a businessman. I want to be known as a man of integrity, who invests intuitively in apartment complexes, and who adds value to others without expecting anything back in return.

> "Even before I knew what I was doing, I was applying the power of affirmation into manifestation, even if it was in the name of a quarrel, machismo, and ultimate street credibility."

I joined a gang in the first place because my biological father was not in my life.

I was just twelve years old.

One of the tasks of my initiation involved a drive-by shooting. All boys seek male role models in some form or another, and on top of that, I also really wanted the bullying to stop. I wanted to be seen as something more than just some kid. I needed that toughness and bravado to protect me from random attacks from predators, even if they were just ten, eleven, or twelve-year-olds like me.

There was this kid that used to bully me in middle school all of the time. He was one of the biggest guys in our school. Most kids were skinny, but this guy was solid and stocky in frame. Back then, cornrows were popular. This bully had his hair braided in short cornrows, and he had two older, bigger, scarier brothers who were in gangs. We all automatically feared them and the bullet, which literally meant an actual bullet to the chest or the head.

This bully was relentless, always kicking me down, throwing stuff at me, knocking things out of my hand, and just pushing me around in general. I was never a coward, though. I never let anyone just punk me, but I think he got away with it more because of who I knew he was affiliated with: the big boy gangs that were as fierce and terrifying as the night. It was either day or night, and if you messed with them, you could bet your life they'd be gunning for you.

And yet at some point in life, even amidst the horrors—you just get tired, and for me—I'd had enough. So on this one particular day, I finally stood my ground, no matter the cost. I'd rather stand my ground and be known for something, even if that meant losing my life—than to be a coward and hide my light just to maintain the so-called "peace."

I jumped into investing in multifamily real estate as an adult, for example, because I got tired of my mother worrying about money, and I wanted to change the negative financial narrative that had plagued my family for generations.

I was walking on the sidewalk around the school when this bully walked up on me and pushed me. I stood my ground, which was even more amazing because he had his two big brothers with him. I remember how tall and muscular they were. I felt like this gave the bully even more motivation to pick on me, showing off his intimidating brothers.

I didn't want to swing at him because I knew the brothers would jump in. Instead, I just kept pushing him back, showing him without words that "I'm not afraid of you." Then suddenly, he pulled a gun on me. It was a revolver.

He aimed and placed the nose of the firearm directly in the center of my face.

That was the first time I'd ever had a gun pulled on me. I could feel the coldness of the barrel, and when it touched my skin, it seemed like it had a mind of its own. My thoughts were instantly seized, and in that split moment, I remember thinking about my mother and my brothers and feeling afraid. I reflected on the meaning and purpose of life itself. But I didn't regret what I'd done. It's weird to have your life flash before your eyes at such a young age. Looking back now, it shifted my perception of life and time, and was my last breath of innocence.

With the gun pointed at me, the bully said, "What you thought this was? You ain't gonna push me around in front of my brothers. I'll smoke you."

Just as the words left his lips, one of his brothers put his hand on his shoulder and said, "Yo, let's go. This ain't working. There are too many people around. They're gonna know it was you if you shoot this kid."

They left, and the blood returned to my face. I'd survived another day. I hadn't backed down, and even though it had nearly cost me my life—I knew I had mentally charted a course that would eventually propel me into an entirely different world. My life had flashed before me. When you taste death and look the grim reaper in the eye multiple times—your perspective on life changes drastically. You get this weird, freeing sensation, knowing you cannot be stopped—and you accept all of the risks and adversities that life brings with a smile.

To survive Chicago, you gotta have heart.

I experience this same whole-hearted passion when I speak to others about why I love real estate and how it has allowed me to make a purposeful impact. My experiences on the South Side of Chicago are my foundation, my roots, a guidebook for my appreciation of life, and reminders of the importance of giving back and adding value to and for others. I don't regret the things I've endured because of the lessons I have learned.

PART II

THE JOURNEY: MY FIRST MULTIFAMILY DEAL

Chapter 1

CONNECTING THE DOTS

"If you don't go after what you want, you'll never have it. If you don't ask, the answer is always no. If you don't step forward, you are always in the same place."
– Nora Roberts

My real estate journey started in San Diego during COVID. Civil unrest and protests were jarring every major city in the U.S. It was a surreal feeling. In the Navy, we'd left the country in peace and returned to turmoil. Toilet paper was out. Stores were being looted. Cities were being burned in anger from the Black Lives Matter movement. And to top it all off, my grandmother had just passed away while I was out to sea on deployment.

Losing her was a hard blow for me. I was primarily raised by my mother and grandmother, so we were extremely close. I resented the Navy and my Commanding Officer for not letting me go home to see her while she was on her deathbed. I wasn't even allowed leave to attend the funeral. My Commanding Officer refused, even though a Red Cross message had come to the ship—all this because he was a racist. He was under five separate investigations for racism and his conduct as a leader. One day he said I could go, but the next, he was assigning me random tasks to complete, holding them over my head as the reason why he couldn't let me go. I completed them all quickly, but even after that, he still came back and said, "No."

I want to point out here that being denied the right to go home and say goodbye to my grandmother was where I truly felt the sharpness, the blade, of having my basic freedoms revoked for no reason other than one man's power trip. I was used to making sacrifices in the military, and I was okay with that. But being at his unfair mercy cut me in a different way. It unlocked something inside me: a PAIN, a ferociousness, a release of the caged human spirit. From there on out, I vowed to myself that I would NEVER be controlled by a man or an organization ever again. I would live as a man of virtue and attain true freedom some other way. And that meant attaining financial success on my own. I just didn't know how that would happen—yet.

This was the main turning point for me.

When I returned to San Diego (where the military had me stationed), I set out to sell the condo I owned in the Otay Ranch submarket. I wanted to use the proceeds to buy a dream home for my family. My goal was to buy a three or four-bedroom home, a place where my mom, stepdad, and brothers could stay while visiting, with plenty of space. I was still thinking like that kid from Chicago, though. I was still thinking small and, unconsciously, derogatorily about myself and my potential. I had yet to meet my higher self or the possibilities of my potential. I had amassed some success but wasn't preparing myself to achieve any type of financial wealth long term.

I put in offers on about six or seven homes, but I lost every single bid. The housing market had always been hot in San Diego, but it was even fiercer with the low interest rates due to COVID. I was starting to get frustrated with all the driving around, losing offer after offer.

The final house my agent and I looked at was in the East Lake area of San Diego, which was somewhat suburban. It was a very nice, peaceful neighborhood with a lot of families in it. I pulled up in my black Challenger Hellcat, getting ready to exit when I got a call from a guy named Ben Rudolph. Ben was a Naval Academy graduate, a real estate investor, and had started a real estate company. I was referred to him through a broker named Mickey Christianson, who'd also started a real estate company. My agent had worked under/for Mickey for a while.

After we exchanged introductions, Ben asked about my background, "Where are you from? What year did you graduate from the Naval Academy? What's your job in the Navy?"

I told him my plan to buy a three-bedroom home in San Diego, and that I was selling my current condo. I mentioned to him I was a Supply Corps Officer, and that I had just returned home after being out to sea for several months.

Ben stopped me excitedly and asked if I knew who Keegan Wetzel was.

I said, "Yeah, I do."

Funny thing, Keegan and I had history. When I first graduated from the Naval Academy, I was selected to serve my five-year commitment as a Nuclear Submarine Officer. Keegan was from Chicago as well. When I later submitted a package for lateral transfer from being a Submarine Officer to a Supply Corps Officer, Keegan wrote me a recommendation. At the time, Keegan was an active-duty Supply Corps Officer for one of the SEAL team units. We had only spoken on the phone but had bonded due to our common Chicago connection. Keegan and I had kept in contact off and on ever since, but it never registered to me or clicked that Keegan was living in San Diego.

Ben said that before I moved forward with buying another house in San Diego, I should talk to Keegan. "Keegan is doing big things with real estate," Ben said.

The next day, I sent Keegan a message on LinkedIn and via email. I wrote, "Hey bro, I talked to Ben Rudolph. He said that you're in San Diego right now, and that you're doing big things in real estate. Let's finally meet in person and connect."

I had no idea what to expect, but Keegan reached back out with, "Great hearing from you, Dre! Sure thing, man. Let's get coffee at the Starbucks in Bay Park."

> "Everything happens for a reason, and all of the dots connect to form a picture. One by one, synchronistic events led me to the next stop, the next person, and the next place on my life journey."

Meeting with Keegan, while sitting at a circular black coffee table outside of Starbucks, we hit it off. He narrated his story of growing up in Chicago, about his parents, and playing football. He told me about how being a Supply Corps Officer in the Navy was good for him, and what he'd learned from the opportunity. Like me, though, he ultimately felt there was a ceiling over his head, and that he really couldn't branch out and grow or be the man of God he felt he was meant to be. We both felt we had a higher calling—something much bigger than ourselves that we needed to do.

Even as a Naval Officer, as a leader of our finest men and women in uniform, I too felt that the military was placing a cap on my potential. I felt that the Navy was halting my ability to break free—and to be who and what I felt God was calling me to be. After hearing Keegan tell his story, I told him mine, including the intimate details of my gang background and how the South Side of Chicago had affected me as a man. I talked about how my mom and grandmother were my WHY, and the constant force that drove every single thing I did.

We bonded further, and then talked shop. I told him about the condo I'd had in Chula Vista, how I'd sold it during COVID, and that I was looking to purchase a dream home for my family. I gave him the history of my actions, putting down offers on homes and losing every one of them. The last home I'd tried for was the one I'd been at when I received the call from Ben. I'd put in an offer $30k over the asking price, thinking I would finally get a yes. Come to find out, that even with $30k over asking, I had submitted the lowest offer.

Everything happens for a reason, and all of the dots connect to form a picture. One by one, synchronistic events led me to the next stop, the next person, and the next place on my life journey. Today, I know that offer was supposed to be rejected. Because if it hadn't been, I wouldn't have become an apartment investor.

Keegan dug deeper and asked me questions about my goals and what I looked to accomplish in the future. I told him about a memoir I'd written, and how I hoped the book would open doors for me—and bring financial opportunities for my family. As I spoke, I began to feel the weight of the frustration I'd been carrying for a long, long time. I badly wanted to break the financial curse over my family. I wanted to be in an economic position where I could just cut a check to my mom and move her out of Chicago.

It was at this precise moment that Keegan made a statement that would forever change the trajectory of my life: "You should buy a multifamily property."

Chapter 2

SYNCHRONISTIC SPARKS

It was as if I'd just seen an alien or a ghost because my face hardened and I looked at Keegan with a crazy expression on my face. "What the hell is a multifamily?" I asked.

Keegan told me that a multifamily property is basically another word for an apartment building, and that they can be classified as small or large. He kept on going, telling me more about how it's defined and what its benefits are as an investment. But I still had a hard time understanding what he meant *precisely* by multifamily property. It just wasn't clicking. I'm a visual learner, and luckily for me—just like that—the next synchronistic spark ignited.

Keegan could see I was struggling, so he mentioned that he owned a triplex multifamily property within Bay Park right down the street. Again, I felt like God was at play (being all-knowing), especially the bit about me being a visual person. Like breadcrumbs on a path, God proceeded to use Keegan in order for me to physically (and fully) grasp the concept that would transform my life forever.

Keegan and I hopped into my Hellcat and drove down the street. We parked in front of a white-paneled property, which had units stacked one on top of the other. When we pulled up, I started laughing to myself. I had been on this street once before. When COVID broke out and I returned from deployment, most gyms in San Diego were closed. However, there was an outdoor gym owned by a veteran named David that was still open.

The first day I went to the gym, I parked on the street right in front of Keegan's property.

There was a gorgeous duplex right next door to it. I remember marveling at how nice the property was. Come to find out, a Naval Academy graduate owned the duplex property. Talk about a small world! It was becoming clearer and clearer to me that it was my destiny to be in front of Keegan's property once again.

Psychology Today defines synchronicity as "a phenomenon in which people interpret two separate—and seemingly unrelated—experiences as being meaningfully intertwined, even though there is no evidence that one led to the other or that the two events are linked in any other causal way." How anyone could have ignored the signs I was receiving would have been a travesty. I was zinging, and I knew that destiny was calling.

Keegan lived on the very top floor of the three-unit property. When we entered his place, we walked straight into the room he had converted into an office space. The apartment was a 3 bed+2 bath unit. Keegan sat down at his computer and opened up the *REDFIN* and *HOMESNAP* real estate websites. He then showed me how to effectively navigate the sites by implementing the filter options, and then how to search for two- to four-unit multifamily properties on the Multiple Listing Service (MLS). I remember how I felt as Keegan scrolled up and down the website pages, and the overwhelming sensation of awe I had at how each property on the screen was listed at $1 million dollars or more. My mind was blown. I thought to myself, *How in the hell am I going to afford a property like this? I don't have a million dollars in the bank.*

Next, Keegan explained that the rental income you receive from each unit can be used to help you qualify for the loan. He even showed me an example of a four-unit property within the Mission Hills submarket of San Diego, which he had considered purchasing before he bought the triplex in Bay Park. We used that property as an example to underwrite (or analyze). Keegan had created a very basic Excel spreadsheet he'd been using to plug in the numbers to underwrite every property. Finally, we used a mortgage loan calculator app on our iPhones to estimate what the total debt service would be.

I left Keegan's place that day with a new mentality about money and real estate. I realized that I had been *thinking small.* Growing up, money was always a concern in our household, and I thought that the best way to build wealth was to invest in stocks and max out my retirement account.

From this point forward, I did things differently.

In the same way I went all in and left gang life behind me when I was presented with the opportunity to attend the Naval Academy—I went all in when Keegan presented me with the opportunity to achieve financial freedom through multifamily real estate.

From there on out, it was off to the races. I was 100% committed to buying a multifamily property, whatever it took. I couldn't stop absorbing information. I was obsessed. I was like a real estate machine, a sponge pulling in information and storing it all like the motherboard of a robot.

> *"All of us, whether or not we are warriors, have a cubic centimeter of chance that pops out in front of our eyes from time to time. The difference between an average man and a warrior is that the warrior is aware of this, and one of his tasks is to be alert, deliberately waiting, so that when his cubic centimeter pops out he has the necessary speed, the prowess, to pick it up."*
> *– Carlos Castaneda*

To operate at maximum efficiency, I created rules for myself that had to be followed no matter what. The first was that when I was in my car, the only thing I would listen to was real estate podcasts—no more music. I listened to podcasts when I worked out. I listened to podcasts in the shower. I listened to podcasts around the house when I was eating, getting dressed, or cleaning. And I bought every single book I could on investing in apartments and read them thoroughly. I read them multiple times and marked the pages with notes and colored highlighters. On top of this, every single day, I analyzed multiple multifamily properties within San Diego. I analyzed anything new that came on the market. I slept, ate, and breathed in the industry.

Keegan later reflected on the day we met in person, noting how quiet I was while he showed me everything in his office. He thought he had scared me away since I wasn't indicating comprehension or responses through social or verbal cues. I told him in response that the whole day was overwhelming. But I was quiet because I was taking in every single thing, processing it and tucking it away in files in my mind. From child to gang member, from student to Navy Officer, and then to aspiring real estate investor—I'd never really observed my unique skill set. The instinctual strength I'd learned from those experiences, mixed with a quiet, observant, high-reaching nature—I started to realized my God-given potential.

(To learn more closed-door insights about the conversation between Keegan and I, and using passion to become a successful multifamily investor, check out *Episode 06* of the *Multifamily By the Slice Podcast.*)

Fast forward from that destined day with Keegan. I absorbed all the information I learned like a superhero discovering his superpowers—and I made it all my own. By analyzing properties every day, I came to know the neighborhoods of San Diego well, and I became familiar with the landscape of the market, and where and how to find good deals. After a while, I learned to build Keegan's basic spreadsheet into something more advanced and efficient. I'd plug in the numbers, and in return, Excel would spit out everything I needed right away, including property insurance and total debt service payments. I was cruising joyfully through my knowledge journey, and I was getting ready to put the information into practice.

After analyzing properties for about two to three months, I put an offer on that same four-unit investment property in Mission Hills Keegan had shown me as an example on his computer. It was listed for $1.4 million. Each unit was a 1 bed x 1 bath mix. The property was located on a hill and had beautiful views of the city of San Diego. I received a counteroffer from the seller a week or two after I submitted my offer. Instead of being excited and moving forward to lock the property down under a contract—I waited. I toured the property with the agent and analyzed the numbers—but I saw little upside potential. The property needed a good amount of work, which wasn't a bad thing.

> "Do you ever just get that feeling, that God gives you—a gut feeling—that it just isn't the right time?"

With each unit being a 1 x 1 unit mix, the units wouldn't have brought in enough income for me to make decent money down the road—even if I upgraded the interiors. I could have accepted the offer and gone into escrow, but—do you ever get that feeling that God gives you—a gut feeling—that it just isn't the right time? God told me it wasn't the time. So, I held off from submitting a counteroffer. I didn't even respond back to the seller. I continued following the divine breadcrumbs that were being laid out for me, and to move on to new properties that came up online.

Chapter 3

PARACHUTE

I went back to the drawing board, analyzing and assessing multi-unit properties every day. Over the course of two or three weeks, I noticed a pattern among many of the multifamily properties within the city: most of the unit mixes were always different. For example, for a triplex, one unit might be a 2 bed x 1 bath while the others were 1 bed x 1 bath. Or consider a neighborhood called North Park, where there might be a 3 bed x 2 bath main house, and a separate structure with a 2 bed x 2 bath unit and a 1 bed x 1 bath in the back. The unit mixes were scattered, and often, this hurt the underwriting of the deal because even in a great, expensive rental market like San Diego—you can only rent a 1 bed x 1 bath unit for so much.

To be an expert in any market, you must analyze hundreds of deals consistently. Over time, neighborhood patterns and inconsistencies will jump out at you. And that's what you focus on and leverage to have an advantage and find a deal.

I saw a lot of great properties, but nothing seemed to work or check out with the numbers. The goal was to find a property that, at a minimum, broke even. This meant the rental income would be enough to cover all expenses. If I could do that, then I knew I could find a decent deal because rental income would always increase over time. If I could do that, the great appreciation from the SoCal market would build me long-term wealth.

Around this same time, I ended up firing my agent. I'd been using the same agent I'd had since trying to purchase a single-family home, which was a mistake. When buying a multifamily property, I quickly learned that you need to work with an agent that specializes in working with real estate investors. This is important. A real estate agent helps you buy a property, yes, but there's a difference between having a realtor who just helps you buy a dream home and an agent who specializes in analyzing a property for profit/investment. They dig deeper into the location, what the rents are, what the upside in appreciation will be, and ways to add to the property to increase its value.

It became very clear fast that the agent I'd been working with didn't know what he was talking about most of the time, and he didn't know how to analyze a multifamily property appropriately. Even more importantly, I was finding the properties to send to him to let him know what I wanted to tour. Not once did he send me something that I hadn't already run the numbers on or had physically driven past myself.

So, I called Mickey Christianson, the Naval Academy grad and broker, and I told him I no longer wanted to work with his agent and that he was fired. Mickey apologized for the inconvenience and promised me he would represent me moving forward in buying multifamily properties. This shift—moving from having an inadequate person on my team to having a person on my team who understood the multifamily landscape and had the right connections—changed the way I was able to fight on the battlefield.

Lesson learned.

Know who you're working with and whether they're pulling their weight. Take the time to cultivate meaningful relationships with the people you do business with. Learn their strengths and weaknesses. Learn what inspires them. And learn what their moral compass is and what integrity means to them. Having the right team members is critical for success in business.

> "The mindset: jump out of the plane and build a parachute on the way down."

I continued to fail at finding any good deals. After two to three more weeks of analyzing properties, on another random, destined day, something in my spirit spoke and said, "Remove the limit on the purchase price filter." I was capping my purchase price at $1.4 to $1.5 million because that was what my loan officer had pre-qualified me for.

I removed the filter and went in with the mentality that if I found something that was above $1.4 million, and it was a good deal, then I'd figure out a way to make it work no matter what.

Read that again.

I'd tap into that Chicago grit that courses through my veins. The mindset: jump out of the plane and build a parachute on the way down.

By removing a price limit on the multifamily properties, a lot more properties became available for me to analyze. It's amazing what you can accomplish and the doors that open for you when you stop placing mental barriers on yourself. For the next few weeks, I continued to assess more listings. Eventually, one property in particular caught my attention: another four-unit in Mission Hills. Technically, it had five units: a 2-bedroom house in the front and in the back, there were three recently built 1 bed x 1 bath units. A garage converted into a studio gave the property a fifth unit. For me, that was the bang for the buck. In addition, the property fell under a piece of legislation in San Diego called "The Mills Act," which meant the front house was considered historic and thus, the property tax received a big discount. I couldn't help but feel excited. This property had many unique aspects that stood out.

Ultimately, that's what you want to look for when purchasing any property: unique aspects (aside from the rental income it generates) that you can leverage to make the property more profitable (or that can add value in the future).

I also loved that the property was in Mission Hills, just a block or two from all the bars there, one block from the main highway that leads into the very desirable neighborhood of Little Italy, and a few blocks walking distance into Hillcrest.

I called Mickey and told him about the property I had found, and I asked him if there was a way I could qualify for a $1.7 million property loan. I straight up said, "What do I have to do to get this deal done and make this thing happen?"

This was the way I'd always thought about things, maybe without even knowing it or realizing it until then. I'd always maintained a NO FAILURE, DO-WHATEVER-IT-TAKES mentality, and all of my inner gusto was being put on the line in those roll-the-dice moments.

Mickey mentioned that he knew a guy who had done a lot of big deals in San Diego, and how he'd taken down some crazy loan packages in the past. Mickey connected me with this mysterious loan officer via phone. After a brief conversation, Tim, the loan officer, told me to send him my financial file. In about a week, he pre-qualified me for $1.7 million—just like that. Somehow, in some seemingly magical way (just like Mickey had said)—he made it happen. Without hesitation, I submitted an offer for the Mission Hills 5-unit property.

The next day while underwriting other new properties on the market, I came across a $1.9 million 4-unit property on a street called Hornblend in the Pacific Beach market. I was enthusiastic about this property because seldom do multifamily properties come online for this location. Pacific Beach is one of the HOTTEST and most desirable places to live within the city. Everyone wants to go there. It's one of the busiest beaches in San Diego, and a lot of young people, young professionals, and people in their 30's and 40's, go there just for the culture and city vibes. There are tons of coffee shops, grocery stores, bars, and an incredibly lively nightlife packed with beautiful, interesting people. Aside from the progressive and flourishing community of Pacific Beach, many aspects about the property itself also stood out to me.

For starters, each unit was a 2 bed+2 bath townhome with its own patio. Every unit was also parcel-mapped, as they call it, meaning that for an exit strategy, I could either sell each individual townhome on its own, or I could sell the entire fourplex. Having a large unit mix like that was rare for a beach community. What I felt was also great about the property was each unit had two parking spots. Again, in a beach community, personal parking is grim.

There were two storage sheds in the back (which could be rented for additional income) and a huge front courtyard at the front of the property. The courtyard had artificial turf, which could easily be renovated to include a Jacuzzi, palm trees, an outdoor fire pit and Cabana, fridge, grill, and bar to really jazz the place up. I saw the potential for increasing rent with added luxuries or putting short-term rentals into place. Each unit was rented for $2,900 a month. When I ran the numbers, the property cash flowed! I got so excited I called Mickey and asked him to meet me in Pacific Beach to walk the property.

> "I said to myself, 'This is my property, and it will be mine.'"

The moment we pulled up to the property and walked around it, I said to myself, "This is my property, and it will be mine." I just knew it. Mickey and I called Tim and asked him if he could stretch again, work his magic, and qualify us for $1.9 million. And just like the last pre-qualification—Tim got me pre-approved for $1.9 million. The only thing I did differently was ask the question; I didn't limit myself or think it was impossible because of the larger purchase price. Without hesitation, I submitted another offer. I knew the property was special and that it was a superb deal.

Chapter 4

INERTIA

I had two offers in motion. Weeks went by, though, and I still had not heard anything back from the sellers' agents. I got concerned. I remember being in the office on base in uniform when I called Mickey and said, "Hey, what happened to our two offers? Why haven't we heard anything back or even received a counteroffer from the sellers?" This was weird, especially because I thought that we were the only people who'd put in offers and they were at asking price.

Mickey said, "Let me find out and give you a call back." Thirty minutes later, Mickey rings and tells me, "The Pacific Beach property received a counter offer. For the Mission Hills property, someone put an all-cash offer on it."

I accepted. I put down $20,000 for an earnest money deposit and the seller credited me $15,000 in closing costs. It was September.

The day I opened escrow, I printed out a colored picture of the 4-unit property, and I taped it to the wall next to my computer. I then took a colored Sharpie marker and wrote the words "This is my property" on it. I needed to constantly visualize my goal and manifest it. Even if I had doubt or didn't fully believe, I needed to trick my mind into believing, and that meant surrounding myself with it.

People don't realize how powerful a vivid goal will help you rise above your challenges.

YOU achieve what you THINK about.

When I entered escrow, everything appeared to move smoothly at first. The inspection report had minor repairs or maintenance concerns. The termite inspection came back clean. And all the lease agreements and rent rolls matched up with what the tenants were currently paying.

I thought I was golden, but soon, disaster struck. Tim became a ghost. I quickly realized how terrible of a communicator Tim was. I was constantly calling him and asking for updates on the loan. He'd been working with three different lenders at the start who'd said they'd fund the deal. However, there was difficulty in funding a $1.9 million Veteran Affairs (VA) loan. There has always been a limit to the amount of the VA loan you can use. When Donald Trump was the president, he removed the cap.

In the eyes of the lenders, there had never been anyone who had successfully completed a $2 million dollar VA home purchase. As far as they were concerned, I was the first person to ever attempt one that big and be successful at it.

Despite what people think, it's not entirely *zero money down* when using a VA loan to buy a small apartment complex. To qualify for the VA loan, and to use it to purchase a multifamily property—you need about three to six months' worth of money reserves for whatever the mortgage payment would be. In addition, the earnest money deposit is about 1-2% of the purchase price. That's quite a bit of money you need to have saved up.

When I finally reached Tim, he expressed the fears the lenders had about the high purchase price. He then asked me if I could have someone else on the loan. Through emotions of irritation and a slight sense of hopelessness, I shot back at him that, "No, I don't have anyone else I can rely on that could be on the loan with me or who would be comfortable with doing so."

I already knew that most people not only wouldn't understand what a multifamily property was, but would also be scared and intimidated by a $2 million dollar purchase price, and having their name on a loan that size.

Throughout the month of October, I felt the pressure of being in a time crunch. I'd already sold my condo in Otay Ranch in September, at which point I'd had to move out. I'd sold it to another veteran and his wife, and they were so nice and understanding of my situation (that I had not closed on my 4-unit property yet), so they worked out a sweet deal with me. They allowed me to keep all my furniture and possessions in their garage. I had all of my stuff stacked and piled on the right side of the garage, they had all their stuff on the left.

The vet's wife was pregnant, so I felt bad they couldn't fully move in after they'd bought the home. I appreciated them and their kindness and empathy (they didn't even charge me for it when they could have). With all of my stuff in the garage, I was living out of my car. One of my other Naval Officer buddies, Tyrise, who lived in Mission Valley, offered to let me crash at his place for a week or two until I closed on the 4-unit in Pacific Beach. I gratefully accepted.

"The tests we face in life's journey are not to reveal our weaknesses but to help us discover our inner strengths. We can only know how strong we are when we strive and thrive beyond the challenges we face."
– Kemi Sogunle

It was November. I crashed on the couch, but it was so uncomfortable to sleep on (one of those really short, hard couches, and I'm a big, tall guy) that I opted to sleep on the floor some nights. It was hard to sleep, and the anxiety about not sleeping contributed to more missed *zzz's*. This didn't help the apprehension I was already feeling about Tim and the lenders. Not too long after Tyrise gave me the green light to stay with him, he received word from the Navy he would unexpectedly be moving because of new short fused orders to Virginia. That gave me a week and a half before the moving company would come to pack up all of his furniture and move him out.

I had just started dating a woman in San Diego, and she knew about my living situation. One day she said, "Hey, you can stay here for a week or two if you'd like. It's really no big deal." What was supposed to be roughly a week or two ended up being a lot longer. I was in escrow until the end of December. I stayed with her while we were getting to know each other and somewhat dating. This was a bit of a strange situation. I was living with her, but I was still kind of living out of my car in a way too. I felt like crap because I'd never been in that type of situation before. I'd always been taught to take care of my priorities as a man, and to not have to rely on others too often or too heavily.

I remember one day in particular feeling very stuck. I was on the couch at this woman's place while talking to Tim on the phone. He reiterated what he'd said to me while I was staying at Tyrise's place. Three to four lenders were supposed to provide me with their approval to finally move forward and lock in my interest rate for the $1.9 million property. However, Tim continued telling me how lenders were still pulling out or pushing back, requesting that I get someone else to be on the loan.

Things were stagnant, and I was feeling the weight of being bogged down by inertia. Why weren't things coming together? What was I missing? How could I realign with that invisible, divine, synchronistic energy that had brought things together for me before? Something needed to change, and that meant reaching out and taking more risks.

I looked down at the tattoo on my left forearm, which reads: "At some point, there is no excuse; either you'll do everything it takes to make it happen, or you don't."

Over the next week or two, I thought more creatively about how to make the deal work. I decided to ask my brother, Alex (who is also a Naval Academy graduate), if he would sign on the loan with me. The bank also wanted someone else on the loan because with a purchase price that big, they said it was risky for them since I had no real estate investment experience. I called Alex and explained my situation to him. He said he was down to support me if it would mean getting approved just by having his name on the loan. Alex sent me all of his information and documents, which I then forwarded to Tim.

Another week ticked by. I still hadn't heard back from Tim. I'd been calling him without getting through. When he eventually did pick up, I casually asked him if he had any updates for me, even though I was screaming for news in my head. "Alex was disqualified by the lender because of some financial troubles he's had in the past," Tim said. This news blew my mind. As my loan officer, Tim failed to call me back and provide any type of update. Or basically, to do his job. I was at a loss, especially that he'd neglected to tell me news that would directly affect whether my loan would move forward to be approved or not.

The way Tim kept me in the dark for a week really, really bothered me. I told him that the way he'd handled the situation was completely unacceptable. In response, he said, "Hey, we still have two lenders left to count on."

Chapter 5

I AM AN ACTIVE CREATOR OF MY REALITY

"Let me not pray to be sheltered from dangers, but to be fearless in facing them."
– Anonymous

One week later, another lender backed out. From there, I was desperately trying to figure out other ways to qualify. Eventually, we nailed down the final lender. It looked like they'd committed to moving forward with my loan package. To get creative to help boost the strength of my loan application, and to not take no for an answer, I did some research and identified a top property management company within San Diego. I contacted them, and after speaking with and vetting them thoroughly, determined they would be a good fit. I then gave the name of the company to the lender to put down on the loan. This would help the lender view my loan application as less risky instead of just having me down as managing the property myself because I had no multifamily real estate experience at the time.

It looked as though I had surpassed another hurdle. The dark clouds of emotional turmoil seemed to clear out and things were moving forward. I regained a steady momentum of hope. Another week or two went by. Mickey and I still had gotten no indication from Tim that he'd ordered the appraisal. This became apparent because I was at work in the office on base when I received a random email and then a phone call from Mickey's assistant. He informed me we had now reached a point in escrow in which I had to sign in order to remove all contingencies.

"If there was any great lesson in life it was this:
No battle was ever won with silence."
– Shannon L. Alder

I was pissed.

I cursed out Mickey's assistant, then got Mickey and Tim on the phone, and cursed them out too. I could feel my take-no-crap-Chicago energy gushing out. I was so, so frustrated by such a severe lack of communication. Mostly because whenever they required anything from me in the escrow process, or they had documents for me to sign—these were things I would take care of right away. But when I asked them questions or for information or updates—it took an unnecessarily long amount of time before I received any response.

This deal was big for me. It could forever change the legacy and course of financial freedom for my family and I. But it looked and felt like no one else was taking it as seriously. Come to find out, my "allies" didn't believe the deal would actually go through.

I was the only one rooting for Team Dre.

Now I had a decision to make: either I sign to remove all contingencies (even though I didn't have the appraisal back yet) or drop out of escrow. I took a leap of faith and trusted that the appraisal would come out fine—so I signed off to remove all of the contingencies and continued moving forward in escrow.

I said another positive affirmation to myself sitting in that office chair, "This appraisal will come back at or above the purchase price." Then I took out a sheet of paper and wrote it down. I needed to force myself to believe it.

Every goal must be written and specific to be achieved.

I doubled down and shifted to a new approach to align everyone and their miscommunication. We did an all hands on deck email I had Mickey send out to Tim, myself, and the underwriter for the lender in order to get everyone on board about getting the appraisal done and the loan approved. It was now November, and we were approaching Thanksgiving.

The first few days leading up to Turkey Day and a few after the holiday, Mickey and I worked with the underwriter, sending him any additional documents he needed and to tie up any loose ends. Tim still hadn't ordered the appraisal yet (because he secretly doubted I'd get approved). Finally, after Mickey had a stern conversation with Tim, we finally had the appraisal ordered.

The appraisal came back $20k more than the agreed-upon purchase price.

I manifested and spoke it into existence.

But don't get too excited yet—the hits kept on coming.

I'd finally reached a point where I felt like we were about to approach the finish line, when all of a sudden, I got a phone call from the underwriter. I was driving down the street when he said those words on the other end of the line.

I had to pull over the car.

"Dre, we need you to come up with another $30k in reserves in order to give the lender the 'warm and fuzzy' that you won't default on the loan."

Plus, it was COVID, so they wanted to be even more conservative. They saw me as a liability because this was my first investment property and because the purchase price was so large. Understandably, I was upset. I remember thinking, *What the hell? You all told me I was good to go, that I'd met all the qualifications, and that the loan was as good as mine. Now you're telling me I have to come up with another $30k? Seriously?* This was like a slap in the face because we were down to the last hour before we were supposed to close.

My mindset was: If I don't do this deal—if I don't—do—something, I'll always be stuck in the same place. I have to do this, and I have to believe that I am an active creator of my reality.

Right after this bullshit occurred, I called my mom and vented to her all of my frustrations about the situation. I felt like my heart was in the right place. I felt like I'd done everything as best I could. I was just a kid from the South Side of Chicago trying to make something of my life, working as hard as I could. The financial curse of my family had to end, and I would be the one to do it. My mindset was: If I don't do this deal—if I don't—do—something, I'll always be stuck in the same place. I have to do this, and I have to believe that I am an active creator of my reality.

I believed in the numbers. I believed in the location. I believed in myself. I called the underwriter and told him there was no way I could just pull $30k out of my ass or ask anyone else to lend it. I told him that my family doesn't come from money, so I couldn't just randomly call and ask them to wire that kind of cash in a matter of days. I also said I felt like this had come out of left field, and that they'd told me I had already met the necessary qualifications. Honestly, it kind of felt like it was all a game for them. Still, he insisted the money be paid.

I told my mother what I was trying to do to make it all work. That's when she uttered words I never thought I'd hear her say.

"Andre, honey, do you think maybe this is all a sign, and that you should just call it quits?"

I ignored the question and kept talking about my motivation behind it all, and how it was something I believed in. This was a seriously earth-shattering conversation, though, because my mom has always been my WHY in life.

What do you do when the main source of your motivation doesn't really believe you can pull off what is needed to thrive?

What do you do when your own family does not support your goals and or dreams?

I'm sure she didn't mean it in that way. She was being a mother, trying to have my back and protect me—but her words still made me take a step back and allowed the process of a new transformation, a new perspective into self-growth.

At that moment, I had to dig deeper and truly believe in myself. Maybe that's why my mother had (unconsciously) said what she had to in order to 100% push me into my own. My inner world became even more convinced by my convictions. I would close this deal, and it would change my life forever—and what still kept me going—was that it would forever change my mother's life too. Closing this deal would give me a $2 million dollar net worth, easily.

Chapter 6

THERE IS ALWAYS HOPE

I was at the gym working out when Mickey called. "Hey, Dre, I think we've hit the wall on this one, man. As your broker, I need to let you know that the seller's agent has informed me that if we don't close this deal—they are going to go after your $20k earnest money deposit. They are really frustrated that we have been extending escrow for so long."

For the next forty minutes, instead of talking about the situation—I focused on talking about how I still believed in the deal and in what I was doing. I'd seen things in my life, in situations that were life and death, both in the gang and in the military. What I'd seen most about life is there are powers that live behind what we can see with our eyes. There are powers or energies that can either push you down or pull you up. Focusing on the higher, loving vibrations can take you from five to five hundred, while focusing purely on the logistics of a situation can only raise you, at most, to a hundred. Even with the potential of losing my $20k earnest money deposit—I still decided to trust in a higher power—and move forward.

Two weeks passed. Mickey talked to the lender and negotiated with them to give me a break on the extra $30k in reserve requirements, especially since we had been through so much in escrow already. It was such a sigh of relief to get the call. I was so happy, and at this point, all we were waiting for were the loan documents.

I had surpassed yet again another major hurdle.

Or so I thought.

Another week went by. Then out of nowhere, the seller's agent behaved belligerently rude towards Mickey, Tim, and me. He was so upset about the closing process and dealing with my loan officer that the next thing I knew, I'd received an email stating that if I did not pay the seller $5,000 to extend escrow another week, plus $500 a day every day after that, escrow would be closed. That $500 a day included weekends, by the way. Like a rollercoaster—my emotions swung again.

We couldn't catch a break.

From September to December, my feelings, thoughts, and pocketbook had been pulled up and down and tossed around by an unpredictable tornado.

You would think I would have just thrown in the towel. My $20k was already on the line. Now, I was being hit with essentially an additional $5,500+ in fees. I had another long conversation with Mickey, after which I stuck with my guns and moved forward by paying the $5,000 plus $500 every day after that.

I know from your perspective that may sound crazy. But I looked at it like this: the wealth I would acquire and build from this deal was worth that little $5k. Plus, I knew that in order to get started in real estate—I *had* to do this deal. I had to start somewhere. I had to do something. It is known as The Law of the First Deal: one deal would forever give me the momentum to move forward and build a portfolio of other properties. I needed this to garner professionalism, and to be seen as serious and legit in addition to the lessons I would learn.

I called my mother once again.

I told her and my stepfather about the extra fines being placed on me, and they both said they felt like this was a final sign from God I needed to leave this deal alone once and for all. They believed I'd been through way too much in escrow at this point, and that, ultimately—it just wasn't worth it. To them, this $2 million dollar deal was an insane amount of money, and I should come back down from the dangers of dreaming of living at such monetary heights.

People are so quick to say that whenever they face adversity, it's a sign from God—and that's simply not true.

My mom had always raised my brothers and me to be respectful, but for the first time ever in my life—I pushed back. I didn't hold my tongue. They were wrong. I knew more about real estate than they did. And more importantly, I knew the San Diego market; I'd been studying it relentlessly. I responded, "No. No. No. You can't say that to me. You can't apply the principle of 'a sign from God' as a failure to this situation when you've applied it victoriously to every other situation in the past. That's not fair."

People are so quick to say that whenever they face adversity, it's a sign from God—and that's simply not true. Adversity and challenges in life do not mean that God is telling you to give up, quit, or walk away.

When my brothers and I applied to West Point and the Naval Academy, we received multiple rejection letters. But my mom never accepted no for an answer. She always challenged them multiple times with her own handwritten letters, with conviction and passion. She ALWAYS fought hard. She ALWAYS fought back. So, how was this any different from how I had responded to my own tribulation?

I dug deep, and I thought about Chicago. I thought about everything that I had been through as a gang member. That animal side: brawling on the streets; the shootings. This instinct-ruled reality is not something many people experience. But for those who have—our physical and emotional senses are heightened. We smell trouble; we smell gullibility; we smell fear. Most who've come from this type of world use this edge to take advantage of people. I choose not to. But I still had the bear's sense of smell, the hawk's sight, the bat's sense of sound, and the dragonfly's antennae. It was the Naval Academy that helped me develop and harness these abilities to do good for the world, for myself, and for my loved ones.

It was down to the wire. All of my life, all of my experiences, everything I was and everything I was meant to be—every single thing was coming down to this deal. Either I went for it and shot for the stars to be financially free—or—I didn't. I had a legacy to live, though, and this deal was something I could pass down to my children that would set us all up for years and years. I wouldn't even have to make another BIG move in life if I didn't want to. Not only that, but the equity, tax benefits, and appreciation I would receive from the property would leverage me to buy future properties.

My next move was clear. I kept pushing forward.

Two weeks passed while waiting for the final documents from the lender. We were approaching Christmas. I was in constant communication with the title company. Any day now and I was supposed to receive a call from the notary to sign documents and close.

Then another barrier was placed in front of me.

I got word there was an issue with the title. We had to wait another few days for the seller and his agent to figure things out on their end. I used this misstep to my advantage. I had the seller and his agent remove the $5,000 I had deposited to escrow plus the $500 a day after that. I argued they had focused so much attention blaming me and my team, when they had actually missed steps too. They agreed to waive the extra fees.

Finally, after a few more days, I received THE CALL.

I signed the documents on my 4-unit property in Pacific Beach on Christmas Eve. I WAS OFFICIALLY A MULTIFAMILY PROPERTY OWNER.

The fact that I closed on Christmas Eve was a sign from God. During escrow, I made a promise to him that if he let this deal work out for my family and me, I would never fail to give him the glory and use real estate to help others.

So here I am.

"No. Don't give up hope just yet. It's the last thing to go. When you have lost hope, you have lost everything. And when you think all is lost, when all is dire and bleak, there is always hope."
– Jobie Hughes (I Am Number Four)

Chapter 7

WHEN VALUE BECOMES REALITY

I shared my story to add value for others, and to show how success can be achieved by ordinary people like you and me—but you must be crystal clear about what you want.

A year later, once I stabilized the property and made improvements, my family came to visit me in San Diego. It was my first time seeing everyone together again since I started my business. I remember how my goal was to buy a dream home where everyone could have a place to stay and feel comfortable.

While they were visiting, they stayed in one of my townhome-style units. What's crazy is that the units are so big that I was able to provide a place for both my brothers (and one of my brothers' dog), my mother, and my stepfather, comfortably. I provided a retreat for them. Looking back, I find it ironic that the name of the 4-unit property on Hornblend is called *The Retreat.* The words are literally printed on a monument sign displayed at the front of the apartment complex.

I provided a retreat for them from the negatives of living on the South Side of Chicago. A retreat from their old way of thinking and how they perceived real estate. A retreat from what they thought was possible and the power of believing in yourself. God still gave me what

I wanted—but in a different way. Instead of just giving me a house, he gave me a business and an investment that would open doors for my family and me.

When my family first pulled up to the 4-unit property and walked around, I remember the look in their eyes. The burning pride. The excitement. Had I listened to my mother and stepfather and quit, we wouldn't have experienced a moment like that. Words cannot express how grateful I felt to give them something. To show them the power of real estate. I would have had to get an overpriced hotel for them in San Diego if I hadn't sacrificed and committed to my dreams. And more importantly, I wouldn't have been able to open their eyes and inspire them.

This was my first true taste of the power in using real estate to create an impact on other people's lives. I did it with my own family.

And now I am doing it for other people.

The lessons I learned being in a gang and closing on the 4-unit property gave me a more defined definition of what true financial freedom means. They include:

1. **INFLUENCE & IMPACT:** For starters, apartment real estate gives me the financial platform to change my immediate family's perspective on money and real estate and allows me to open more doors for them—that in their own strength—they couldn't do. Second, I could combine outreach with multifamily real estate. I could host outreach events at properties. I could organize field trip tours to various properties. Improving properties also directly uplifts and brings good to a community. I could also leverage real estate with motivational speaking to help inspire youth and others to think bigger about how to invest their money smartly. I might not be able to change the world, but my actions might spark and motivate the mind of the person that will. God gave me the voltage and the opportunity to invest in multifamily real estate, so now I have to use it to give back.
2. **BUYING A SINGLE-FAMILY HOME IS NOT THE WAY:** My mindset has now shifted about how I view the sin-

gle-family home. I'm not saying I will never buy a single family, but if I do, it better have an additional unit (ADU) that I can either build or that is already present I can rent to offset a percentage of my mortgage or that would cover my debt service entirely. Bare minimum, I would prefer a large duplex, where I could live in the top unit and guests could live at the bottom. Multifamily investing has made me look critically at a property and how it can be used for income. There are short-term rentals to consider as well, but that is a different niche within real estate. Even then, you should NEVER buy a short-term rental property that if you had to place a long-term tenant within it for a year or longer, the rental income wouldn't be able to cover your entire mortgage payment.

3. **USE YOUR SUPERPOWER TO ADD VALUE:** If I no longer have to worry about money, I now have the freedom to shift my attention to using my gifts and talents to give back to the world. Whether that be through art, education, the military, nonprofit work, sports, etc.

If I could sum all this up and put it in an equation, it would be this:

Value = Education x Passion x Hustle

In retrospect, I have always been an ambitious, driven, risk-taker type of person. But closing on that $2 million dollar 4-unit property taught me how to be fearless and believe in myself in a different capacity. It taught me we have to trust our intuition, and that we have to trust our relationship to the good energy in life. It was hard at times. I realized others didn't trust in my vision, and that they simply couldn't understand it. But those experiences were liberating. Because my inner, spiritual world suddenly became the most trustworthy thing in the world. Self-doubt is no longer something I have to grapple with.

I had done it. I'd made it. My life was beginning, and I was on the road to successful longevity. Being at this point in life is eye-opening. Being in the present of where you'd always hoped to be makes you think. I've been through Joseph Campbell's Hero's Journey. I've done it three times: my life in a gang, my life as a Naval Academy graduate and Officer, and my life as a real estate investor. With each journey, I departed from the ordinary world and crossed a threshold into a new adventure, each made up of its own percentage of light and darkness. I heard the call of adventure strongest when I joined the military, knowing I was heading into something that was going to genuinely help me become stronger and better. I was tested by enemies, and allies, and through my challenges, I climbed higher and obtained new growth.

> *"The journey of the hero is about the courage to seek the depths; the image of creative rebirth; the eternal cycle of change within us; the uncanny discovery that the seeker is the mystery which the seeker seeks to know. The hero journey is a symbol that binds, in the original sense of the word, two distant ideas, the spiritual quest of the ancients with the modern search for identity, always the one, shape-shifting yet marvelously constant story that we find."*
>
> *– Joseph Campbell*

There was always an ordeal and an epiphany that eventually came, a rebirth that pushed me forward. The great adversary, self-doubt, was defeated time and time again by self-love and fearlessness. The reward of trusting in God and the universe brought ultimate resurrection, whereby the shifting from self-doubt to self-respect ended. And from there on out, my ordinary world no longer contained self-distrust. The journeys had changed me, and there was no going back. There is no going back now—but many, many new adventures lay ahead.

Chapter 8

APPLYING GANG LIFE TO REAL ESTATE

Being in a gang taught me a lot . . . the first advantage was that it taught me how to read people.

Being in a gang taught me a lot in terms of how to succeed in real estate. The first advantage was that it taught me how to read people. When you're a gang member, you're constantly aware of your surroundings, people's body language, how people talk, how their hands move, how they dress, etc. Now working in a field in which I'm constantly interacting with so many investors, so many business-minded people—my ability to read them is immediate; it's instinctual. Within a split second, I've assessed a person's character, personality, and intentions, all just by the way they carry themselves.

This learned ability translates well in business because even in real estate, there are a lot of wolves with ulterior motives. Or shady people you should stay away from and not get involved with financially. In real estate, you will partner with people on various things. It could be any type of deal or partnership: it could be speakers, a recording and/or podcast, a meetup, property managers, appraisers, lenders, interior designers, the list goes on—there are many different relationships you can find within the industry. Whatever the partnership may be, the ability to assess someone's character quickly on the fly is a highly advantageous asset.

Being in a gang taught me how to hustle with hunger.

Everything moves fast in a gang world. Your adrenaline, your nervous system, even your hormones—they're JACKED all the time. It's fight or flight every day. It is cortisol levels CRANKED to the max, as each step you take on the South Side of Chicago is a constant reminder of death waiting at every corner. Being in a gang taught me how to *hustle with hunger*—and I had to tap into that hustle, and I had to tap into that hunger—to eventually escape the gang.

I frequently remind myself of this today. It's hard not to forget it because I know what my life used to be like, and I value where I am at. But through constant reminders, I know what I have to do to make it, and what I can teach others to do if they also want to get to where they want to be. You have to get up early. You have to stay up late. You have to constantly chase the worm, as they say: analyzing deals, looking at properties, communicating with investors, etc. So, the ability to constantly hustle and out-hustle everyone else has served me well. I always want to be the hardest worker in the room, and I've always sought excellence in some way or another.

People are amazed at my stamina and perseverance. I'm often asked how in the world I'm able to balance and manage being a Naval Officer while operating my own real estate business. My time is even more crunched because I'm working not only a technical job, but I also have the responsibility of leading people and taking care of their livelihood as an Officer. I'm able to balance all of this because I hustle—I hustle HARD and FAST.

I get up at three or four in the morning, and I use my one-hour lunch break to work my real estate business. When I get off work, I go to the gym for an hour and a half. The rest of the night, plus my weekends—I'm working on my business. I'm making time. My drive is raw and intense, and I thrive on it. I never make excuses. I enjoy the climb, and I have plenty of energy to keep pursuing amazing heights.

Whether it's inhaling podcasts or hunting for new creative ways to absorb and gain knowledge about real estate—it's a never-ending thirst, and the labor keeps me hydrated.

I've seen the other end of the tunnel and had multiple dances with death. Helping my family and others earn wealth through real estate is a blessing.

The ability to articulate words in just the right way is essential for survival in any gang—because you have to smartly navigate past, around, and through other people to avoid negative outcomes.

Being in a Chicago gang also taught me how to be smooth. I had to know how to talk into, talk out of, use straight talk, pep talk, talk big, and talk heart-to-heart. I had to soften edges, and effectively use language that simultaneously threatened enemies and stood my ground while also not escalating a situation out of proportion. The ability to articulate words *in just the right way* is essential for survival in any gang—because you have to smartly navigate past, around, and through other people to avoid negative outcomes. This innate ability probably saved my life because I knew many people, who, due to their anger, big mouths, or pride—were killed. I have learned to be an expert at being calm and learning how to diffuse situations.

In real estate, I can expertly speak and engage with people, and I know how to draw out people's passionate points and motivations. This is critical for raising capital and building relationships. Being a former gang member has also allowed me to become an expert negotiator. I can eschew conflict while simultaneously effectively holding my ground. With kindness hinged on instinctual power, I'm not perceived as a punk OR as a pushover. My stance is founded on reason and authenticity.

My mind was triggered into thinking up, higher, over—OUT OF.

The gang life taught me how to see the big picture and think outside of the box. Because so many young people are killed due to gun violence, the main perception of survival was that "The odds are stacked against me," or, "I hope I make it." This conjured early existential questions. I took the approach of looking at my environment with questions such as: *Why not me? Why not this? What if this?*

I have witnessed a lot of violent and terrible things on the streets. Because of those horrible situations and the things I endured, I had an opposite response to them. Perhaps it was an innate spirituality or intellectualism that helped me process realities differently. But somehow, those traumas actually triggered my brain to think differently. I guess you could say I responded to an animalistic environment philosophically.

My mind was triggered into thinking up, higher, over—OUT OF. I thought, *what would life be like if it wasn't this?* Instead of being complacent and accepting the mindset that my life was what it was, and that I would most likely die young—I mentally transformed those ultimatums. I said NO, I will not accept this. Gang life forced me to ask deep life questions. It made me become a visionary, uplifted by opportunities, dreams, goals, and a transpersonal view of life. This ability to zoom out and see the big picture has only amplified my perceptions in the real estate industry.

Be different—and be proud of it.

Being in a gang taught me to be different—and be proud of it. Gang member to Naval Academy graduate has definitely put me in a unicorn-type category. I'm not afraid to be different or to stand out. My uniqueness is what made it possible to escape the gang and inspire other members in the gang as well. That's a powerful impact, and to this day, I hold it in high regard. My story is unusual and diverse, and I suppose that's my advantage. This is because as I continue to build my business, I have no desire to be like or do it like anyone else. For example, everyone usually uses the same structure when naming their business: it's their last name followed by capital or something synonymous to this, like Evans Capital or Johnson Investment Group. I'm not taking a jab at or criticizing those with these types of business names. Yes, they sound professional—but there's nothing unique about them that stands out.

I made the name of my business *That's My Property*. The logo is a sticky note with the Chicago skyline in the center and a thumbtack holding the sticky note in place. The sticky note itself is a symbol for writing down the goals you want in life as affirmations that lead to manifestation. The name of the business itself, *That's My Property*, is an ongoing, positive manifestation. Imagine going up to every property or potential deal and saying to yourself, "That's my property." In this way, the name of my business works double, on the material realm, and the spiritual.

I wanted a name that brought light out of people and inspired them, and studies have shown that when you write something down (especially goals), you unlock a different part of your brain that allows you to process things differently. Your brain will naturally figure out ways to accomplish whatever the goal is. I wrote down my goals and what I wanted out of life like this when I was in the gang. I wrote down affirmations such as, "I'm going to get out of Chicago." And now I write them for my business goals. Affirmations are a positive and powerful way of speaking intentions into existence. They make challenges easier and inspire us to be and do better.

Chapter 9

NAVAL ACADEMY STANDARDS IN REAL ESTATE

"FEAR = A GPS for where your soul most wants to go."
– Anonymous

Honor & Integrity: An advantage of being a Naval Academy graduate is the acute awareness of and use of integrity. This is a rare quality in business and real estate, yet it's the most valuable.

I cannot emphasize that enough.

At the Academy, we were taught to adhere to a high code of honor called the Honor Concept. It states:

Midshipmen are persons of integrity.

They stand for that which is right.

They tell the truth,

And ensure that the truth is known.

Integrity is always more important than the deal in real estate. Investors can be sure that because of my background as a Naval Officer and Naval Academy graduate, their capital investment is safe and will be treated with the highest standard.

Out at sea or in the field, U.S Navy sailors' parents and loved ones demand that of me too. I was taught to take care of my people, and to place their needs above mine, which even extended to something as simple as eating last as a leader. That means there may be days where I barely ate—but that's what it means to be called to serve as a leader.

In this same vein, It is my duty to communicate the good and the bad to my investors about every aspect of a multifamily deal.

Professional/Inclusive/Adaptable/Courageous: My training and education of adapting quickly under pressure, and inspiring a team to perform with excellence, all started in Annapolis. One of the most notable positions I had was being the Plebe Summer Regimental Commander. I was the highest-ranked midshipman in charge of leading over 5,000 people.

I was just twenty-one years old.

I have obtained the ability to manage teams effectively (which applies when working with business partners, contractors, or property management) and being detailed/systems-oriented. In the military, it's constantly jammed down our throats to have systems/processes in place. We are taught to be forward thinking and to consider what could potentially go wrong. If one thing falls through, we must be able to quickly adapt to respond appropriately to adversity. Being a Naval Officer and Naval Academy grad strengthened my resolve to stay calm under pressure. In real estate, it's valuable to be able to anticipate what could go wrong in a deal. Because things will go wrong—and the ability to stay calm and still be adaptable during adversity is critical. These traits have led me to clarify business decisions when leading teams of people.

Selflessness: At the Naval Academy, we were taught to place the needs of the nation, the Navy, our peers/classmates, and our subordinates above our own personal recognition or reward. This translates to real estate in the management of investors' hard-earned money. My team and I will always be good stewards of our investors' capital and place their needs before our own no matter what.

PART III

OUR JOURNEY: MULTIFAMILY REAL ESTATE EDUCATION

Chapter 1

MULTIFAMILY REAL ESTATE EDUCATION

You have now seen my beginnings, my journey, and the special skills that have allowed me to succeed. Now we will get into the meat and potatoes for those of you who wish to pursue apartment investing. What is required is that you reset and raise your expectations of yourself and what you think of financial freedom. It's my turn to teach. We're going to go over a few things that will help you make the right decision for you. I look forward to collaborating with you in the future.

Are you ready to commit now? If you have made the decision right now to move forward and would like to invest in multifamily real estate, then visit my website (drmultifamily.com) and book a call with me.

If you haven't done so already, I encourage you to check out the free goal planners attached to the back of this book. I hope they add tremendous value to you. Fill them out and send them to me, and let's go through them together on our call.

Let's Get Real About Why We Are Investing In Real Estate In The First Place

Ask yourself: What is financial freedom to you? How do you feel and what do you envision when you think about real estate? What is life really about? What do you really want? Is it money you want, or is it what money can provide?

Financial freedom is when all of life's basic expenses are covered through passive cash flow. This is achieved when your money works for you and generates income even when sleeping, traveling, or relaxing.

After speaking with and interviewing countless people on my podcast and through my networking group, I have found that what most people want is the freedom that real estate provides, without the desire to be involved actively in the day-to-day operations of it all. My job is to help you determine how much money you must invest in our multifamily deals so the cash flow the properties produce covers all of your expenses.

When I was a midshipman at the Naval Academy, there was a sweet little Christian lady who was a cook in the kitchen. Every time she saw me, she would give me a big hug and say words of wisdom or motivation. The morning of the day I graduated, she said something to me that I'll never forget: "Everyone has twenty-four hours. It's what you use it for that matters. I'm so proud of you, Dre. You used your time to master all you could during your four years here, and you helped others at the same time."

Thus, time is what matters in life. It's the only thing we can't buy or get more of. What most of you are really after is a Return on Time (ROT).

Think about it.

Why would we sacrifice the most useful and joyous years of our lives with parents, kids, growing up, learning, etc., just to work to exhaustion to have a large enough nest egg to live off of for retirement?

Without the worries and stressors associated with money, there is a way we can spend our time with the people we love and care about. We can spend our time traveling, relaxing, engaging in community outreach, pursuing our passions, and using our gifts and talents to help others. We can use this new time to focus on impact.

Here's how.

"Wealth is not about how much money you have in the bank account; wealth is all of those moments that we can't get back."
– Sophia Bush

Chapter 2

THE SHOWDOWN: THE STOCK MARKET VS. MULTIFAMILY

For decades, financial advisors and Wall Street have jammed down our throats that the stock market is the best way to invest for lucrative returns. Most financial advisors take, on average, an annual 1% assets under management fee for taking your capital and placing it in investment funds that are designed to track the stock market. However, once these advisors are paid their fee, many of you will achieve returns below the market at a loss.

As a kid growing up on the South Side of Chicago, I watched my parents invest in the stock market for years—and they still have nothing to show for it. They have not achieved any significant wealth. It's for this reason I've sold my entire stock portfolio, and why I feel it is my duty and moral obligation to help people invest in recession-resistant, high-yielding assets like multifamily syndications.

Let me be straight up with you.

The stock market is not the best way to achieve passive income. To add to this, on any day, at any moment, all your hard-earned income and years of portfolio growth can be erased due to how easily the stock market is affected by market volatility. The value of stocks can shift negatively from legislation, the actions and statements of corporate tycoons and politicians, twitter, or just mere rumors.

Why would I want the value of my stocks to rise or fall just because Elon Musk walked outside in his boxers and commented about a certain company?

I don't know about you, but I don't want my money at the mercy of various random swings and unpredictable factors.

That's not true investing.

There has to be a better way to invest for more reliable, stable, lucrative returns. We owe this to our family and loved ones counting on us.

And the answer is here in this book.

I said it before during *PART I* of the book. But let me repeat it again. Simply put, multifamily is just another word for apartments. Multifamily real estate is any property with two or more housing/dwelling units. Historically, since the 1950s, people have received an average annual return of 6% to 8% from the stock market. In comparison, multifamily property investments have yielded 17% to 25% on average. Multifamily has also been resilient in economic downturns and recessions, and they are the fastest to bounce back compared to any other investment class.

There are a few key reasons multifamily real estate has been resilient as an investment class:

1. **Stability**. Multifamily is not influenced by stock prices, market indices, or consumer confidence within the economy.
2. **A necessity for survival.** Regardless of the income you make—food, water, and shelter are the three most basic human needs. Having a place to live is an unavoidable necessity. People will always need a place to live, even during a recession. In addition, even during a market downturn or financial hardship, people prioritize making their rent payments over paying for other things like cars, credit cards, clothes, etc.

3. **Demand is skyrocketing.** Now, more than ever, people are choosing to rent and live in apartments. Millennials and baby boomers especially hate being tied down to paying a mortgage payment. They love the flexibility of picking up and traveling to various cities to work and live. According to the National Multifamily Housing Council, the U.S. needs to build over 328,000 apartments per year to keep up with the demand in population migration and immigration. America has struggled to meet this metric. And we won't. In short—multifamily housing is in hot demand and will continue to increase.

4. **Inflation protection.** On average, inflation rises at a Fed rate of about 2%. Multifamily properties, which rise in value from appreciation and the cash flow they produce, increases on average at 3%. Thus, apartments are a great hedge against inflation. What's even crazier is that it is inflation itself that drives the increase in equity in the value of apartments and the ability of owners to increase rents. In a funny way, inflation is bad or negative for other investment classes but positive for multifamily.

5. When you sell stocks, you are taxed 100% on the long- or short-term capital gains you received. In multifamily real estate, you can pay little to no tax from profits. In syndications specifically, the money LP investors receive back from refinance or sale is considered return of capital and not capital gains. In addition, the IRS does not allow you to depreciate stock investments. In multifamily real estate, a major tax benefit is your ability to depreciate the property across 27.5 years and accelerate that depreciation through something called cost-segregation (more on this later).

Chapter 3

WHAT ARE THE DIFFERENT TYPES OF MULTIFAMILY?

Every journey starts somewhere. Just like in the movie *Transformers*, where 18-year-old Charlie Watson discovered a beat-up Volkswagen Beetle that actually turned out to be a hero robot named Bumblebee, multifamily properties are all around us full of hidden potential. They can come in many flavors, shapes, and sizes. By definition, small multifamily is considered 2 to 4 units, while large multifamily is considered 5 units or more. I like to break apartment buildings down into 15 categories:

1. **High-rise:** We typically think about this when someone says multifamily. A large complex with 10 or more stories in an urban city setting.
2. **Mid-rise:** An apartment building with an elevator and 5 to 10 stories.
3. **Garden Style:** The most popular style of apartment building located in urban, suburban, and rural populations. They range from one to three stories tall, with each unit having an exterior entrance, and most units have a balcony or patio. Class B and

Class C properties are the most common classifications for garden-style apartments.

4. **Side by Side:** Complexes with units located side by side with one shared wall. This is common among duplex, triplex, and fourplexes. Tenants like side-by-side units because it eliminates the noise complaints of having someone live above or below them. Many of these side-by-side apartment complexes can have townhouse-style units that mimic a detached home with a private entrance, which tenants like as well. Landlords love side-by-side complexes because it's easy to split utilities among tenants.

5. **The Large House**: One massive house, somewhat like a college dormitory, where there are multiple dwelling units located within. Tenants do not have a separate entrance. These unique large house multifamilies are created by a landlord remodeling and configuring the large home in a way to add in or space out rooms into units. Some units will have their own individual kitchen, or sometimes one or two large kitchens shared by all the tenants. Although large house multifamilies typically yield great returns in cash flow, they are often subject to zoning, legal, and permitting issues. Because of this, many lenders and or property management companies may not be willing to lend on or manage these property types.

6. **Micro Cottages**: Many little homes located or grouped together on one lot or street. Each cottage is identical and is a stand-alone house. Tenants like these properties because it feels like a single-family home, with no shared walls, and offers more privacy.

7. **LEGO Stack**: Just the way it sounds, this is when a complex has units stacked on top of one another. This is most commonly found with duplexes. These apartment styles are easy to rent and offer great cash flow. The downside is that tenants live above or below one another and could complain about about noise.

8. **Additional Dwelling Units (ADUs)**: This style of unit has become popular in cities like California. ADUs can be added to a single-family home to create a multifamily, added to an existing multifamily structure to create even more units, or built on a

single large lot for multiple units. What is unique about ADUs is how they can be constructed. ADUs can be built from the ground up, or they can be designed using the existing structures on a property such as garages, basements, laundry rooms, attics, courtyards, etc.

9. **Mixed-use:** An apartment building used for multiple purposes. It's common to have a commercial space on the bottom floor (with multiple units on the top), or a commercial space in the front of the property with residential units in the back.
10. **Hotel conversion:** Small to large hotels converted into multi-family units for long-term leases or short-term rentals.
11. **Student Housing:** Apartments of various unit mixes and styles used to house student tenants.
12. **Senior Living Housing:** Apartment of various unit mixes or styles used to house senior citizens.
13. **Condominium Units:** Apartment buildings converted to condominium ownership where residents own their own individual units but share the common areas.
14. **Loft style:** Units converted from a building that used to be an industrial space. This is common in markets like Providence or Boston.
15. **Prefab:** Prefabricated apartment unit modules built and manufactured in a factory and later assembled at the building site. These styles of units are more affordable and are common in cities like San Francisco. Prefab apartment buildings are typically several stories high.

Chapter 4

SO, WHAT IS A SYNDICATION?

Why risk your hard-earned money in the stock market, which is basically legalized gambling? Why not invest in a high-yield investment like apartment syndications instead?

When I was a kid, every time I went to the movies, I would mix all the flavors of the ICEE machine into one large cup. A little bit of grape. A little bit of red cherry flavoring. A splash of green apple. Then mango. And last, a touch of the Coca-Cola flavor. The result was an ultimate ICEE with all these colorful flavors combined that was better than the individual flavors themselves. I still continue this tradition today.

Syndication is similar to this too; it's when a group of investors come together with their money to buy a large asset such as an apartment building. You can syndicate anything: a candy bar, a jet, a yacht, a football team, or even a bag of potato chips. Imagine asking a group of your buddies each for $1 to buy a $4 Hershey's Cookie 'N' Cream candy bar. In exchange for your friends providing you the money to buy the delicious chocolate, you promise to give them a regular return on their investment. There is a shortage of Hershey bars in the world, as a result, the value of the candy rises after 3 weeks. You sell the chocolate bar and double the money your investor friends gave you at $2 apiece.

Of course, no one will syndicate candy or a bag of chips, but you get the point.

A syndication allows sponsors (or partners) to purchase a large commercial property they typically could not purchase by themselves. The investors receive a lucrative return on their money and amazing real estate tax benefits.

I urge you to take a moment and look at the large multifamily properties within your own neighborhood or city next time you are driving around. Now ask yourself: How would you feel if you were part owner in that property?

Really imagine that.

And all you had to do was contribute about $50,000 to do so. Now that's pretty cool. Investing in a multifamily syndication is like a stock market investment, but with a significantly larger upside.

I help people preserve or generate wealth by offering them opportunities to invest in multifamily syndications.

Below is a list of other common commercial real estate assets that are syndicated:

- Self-storage
- Mobile Home Parks
- Medical Office Buildings
- Multifamily
- Hotels
- Wineries
- Stadiums
- Development Properties
- RV Parks
- Retail Properties (laundry, grocery, mail, nails, hair)
- Industrial Warehouse Properties (think Amazon)

The holding period for a syndication project is usually between three to seven years. During this time, the goal is to maximize the cash flow the property generates by raising rental rates. This is achieved by improving property management and increasing the value of the property through interior and exterior upgrades. This concept of improving the property through renovations is called Value Add, which we'll discuss further later in the book.

Syndications are private placement investments and are regulated by the Securities and Exchange Commission (SEC) through Regulation D: 506(b) & 506(c). Investing in a syndication deal is like being a part of an exclusive club. One reason that many people don't even know about the powerful opportunities that syndications offer is that there is a limited amount of information available on the topic. It used to be that investing in syndications was a best-kept secret only among the ultra-wealthy. In addition, the subject itself can seem complicated and intimidating for many.

I'm here to change that in this book.

My goal is to ensure that you as an investor thoroughly understand all the mechanics behind apartment syndications so you can determine if this investment opportunity is a good fit for you and your family. If you have any questions at any time, reach out to me at drmultifamily.com and let's talk about it.

Chapter 5

HOW IS A SYNDICATION STRUCTURED?

V*room! Vroom! Vroooooooom!* The Nascar race car briskly turned the corner and pulled into its pit stop area for a quick service maintenance. Like a bunch of worker bees, a group of crew members came flying out to change the tires, check fluids, and make sure everything about the vehicle was good to go. If someone fails to do their job properly, it will greatly affect the driver's ability to win the race. Or worse, could even kill them. The driver must truly trust that the pit crew is taking care of him or her by making the appropriate changes and adjustments to the car.

There are two main roles within a syndication: (1) The Limited Partners and (2) The General Partners.

- □ **Limited Partners (LP) (aka Passive Investors):** Those interested in investing passively in real estate syndications. This means they contribute their money to purchase a selected target property. They do not sign on the loan, cannot be sued, and are not responsible for managing the day-to-day performance and operation of the property (hence, the term limited). In return for contributing their capital, Limited Partners receive equity (are part owners) in the apartment complex, and they receive cash flow distributions from the rental income and depreciation tax benefits without actually doing any work. This rental income is also termed what some consider mailbox money. Because Limited Partners have equity shares in the deal, when the property is sold, they receive a portion of the profits from the sale if it has appreciated in value.

Their role is limited because if they had a say or vote in matters, then the property could not be operated effectively.

The majority of the investors in a syndication may not have the knowledge of how to operate a business or multifamily investment. Thus, another reason LP(s) have a limited role is that you do not want to give decision-making opportunities to an individual or group of individuals just because they contributed more capital than you (thus a larger ownership percentage in the deal). That would give them the ability to make a decision that affects your money as an investor. Having the GP(s) make overall decisions on how the syndicated property is run and managed is a structure that protects the LP investors too.

- ☐ **General Partners (GP) (aka Active Investors):** Are also called Sponsors, Syndicators, or Operators. The GP(s) find the apartment building, analyze the deal, get it under contract, and manage the property's business plan from start to finish to ensure it succeeds. GP(s) are responsible for the debt obligations of the property and all legal concerns. They also coordinate and ensure the LP investors receive monthly or quarterly payment distributions on the money they invested. This requires a ton of time and effort, which is where I come in.

General Partners are like the Nascar pit crew that are experts at knowing everything about the racecar and how it operates. Limited Partners are in the car. All they have to do is put their hands on the steering wheel and enjoy the exhilarating ride. The work that the GP(s) did to the car to manage it will accelerate the LP(s) forward down the track toward building financial wealth. It's a relationship balance built on trust.

Now that we have explained a syndication is when a group of people gather their money together to purchase an asset such as an apartment building, and the roles involved, let's look at an example.

Picture this: you have $50,000 within your bank account. You have a couple of options here. You could take that money and buy a turnkey rental property (which would produce lower returns than a syndication with less upside) or you could dedicate a significant amount of time analyzing rental properties, completing initial inspection tours, qualifying for a loan, closing, managing the tenants, and then operating the property to get it to cash flow. If the property needs to be repositioned in a significant way, such as money needed to complete repairs or renovations, then managing contractors and repairs will take time to complete as well. What if you inherit tenants that cause problems? What if you find other mechanical issues such as plumbing or electrical are bad right after closing?

And this is where people turn away and realize that running an investment property can take a great deal of sweat equity. It sounds cool to say you solely own an investment property, but many do not want the work that comes along with it.

Real estate syndications are the alternative that allows hard-working, good people to get into real estate without giving up their time and or experiencing headaches to do so.

There is a reason why for decades, syndications have been the preferred method where the wealthy invest their money. I can't say that enough. Let's consider another example, but this time involving an apartment syndication itself.

Imagine this: there is a team of 2 or 4 syndicators working together to find an apartment complex to buy in San Diego. At least one of the Operators lives in the city, so he or she is the boots on the ground that works with multifamily brokers to tour and find a property that meets specific criteria. After a period of time reviewing multiple apartment buildings, the broker and on-site Operator find a 20-unit apartment listed for $4.5 million.

Another one of the team members then digs deep into underwriting (their superpower or specialty) the 20-unit property by reviewing its rental income and expenses. After careful, conservative analysis of the financials, it is concluded the property has a large amount of upside potential and is worth purchasing. They submit a letter of intent (LOI) to purchase the complex. It is accepted by the seller.

Now, the team of syndicators does not have enough money to purchase the 20-unit apartment building on their own. So they work with an attorney to create a proper syndication offering, finalize the business plan for operating the complex, and create a professional investment summary and pitch deck to present to Limited Partner investors.

Each passive investor invests at least $50,000 into the syndication opportunity. The team of syndicators raise enough capital to cover the down payment and renovation costs and successfully close on the deal.

Another one of the team members has a construction background (another individual superpower) and uses that to estimate and manage the exterior and interior renovations conducted on the 20-units. The team also works alongside the property management company to improve the operations, communicate with tenants, and manage the schedule of completed renovations.

The moment the team of General Partners closes on the deal, they send out regular monthly or quarterly cash flow distributions via ACH to all their passive investors.

The Limited Partner investors are happy and jump for joy at being part owners in a large apartment complex in sunny San Diego while receiving passive income without doing any work.

Fast forward: the Sponsors have now owned the property for 3 years. They decide it's a great time to sell and end up selling the apartment building for $9.5 million. They return all the investors' initial capital. Then, they split the profits from the sale 80/20 with the passive investors.

The passive investors more than doubled their initial investment amount, received regular cash flow distributions, and received yearly tax benefits during the lifecycle of the apartment deal.

They are so happy they start doing cartwheels in the street and tell other friends about the amazing syndication team. On the next apartment deal, they invest again.

"YOU *have the potential to greatly influence many people's lives in a positive way. And if you don't realize that potential, then you're being a little selfish because you're not giving to others and helping them reach their financial goals. Which, by the way, will help you reach yours too (and then some).*"

– Joe Fairless

Chapter 6

HOW DO I KNOW IF I WANT TO BE A LIMITED PARTNER?

In the movie *The Pursuit of Happyness*, Will Smith is in search of finding himself, a consistent salary, a decent home, and a family. He and his five-year-old son live on the streets while he fights to discover the true values that matter in life. Will had no one to ask him the right questions or guide him on his journey of discovery.

I'm here to help you find your meaning as a real estate investor.

We all agree that real estate is a great thing. There are numerous cash flow and tax benefits. However, many hard-working individuals believe they have to do so actively, and that's just not true.

To determine if passive investing is the best approach for you, ask yourself these questions:

1. Are you afraid of the stock market?
2. Are you tired of low returns from other investment vehicles?
3. Did you recently sell your home or a property, and are looking to roll funds into another asset class for diversification?

4. Do you recognize the power of real estate, but are you busy working a full-time job?
5. Are you busy being a parent or traveling?
6. Do you want to receive the benefits of being part owner of a large apartment complex, but don't have the money, experience, or time to purchase one on your own and/or you don't want to incur the credit or liability risk?
7. Do you want to enjoy retirement or obtain another care-free passive income stream?
8. Do you want to receive all the tax benefits of investing in real estate without actively looking for, analyzing, and assessing deals?
9. Do you want to invest in an opportunity with low risk?
10. Are you busy helping others through outreach and community service?
11. Do you believe wealth is found in real assets and not paper instruments?
12. Do you have a habit of buying and selling investments often, which results in high transaction costs?
13. Do you like the feeling of helping others, improving a community, and/or providing housing?
14. Do you like to feel in control of your life and the investments you place your money in?
15. Do you have an issue with big business politics and legislation?
16. Do you fear or have concerns that the current returns you are receiving from other investment vehicles will not be enough to support you during retirement?
17. Do you need immediate cash flow to pay off any expenses?
18. Are you interested in the preservation of your capital?
19. Are you looking for a way to smartly defer capital gains?
20. Do you want to receive all the benefits active real estate investors gain without putting in the same work?

If you answered "YES" to any of the above questions, then investing passively would be the best option for you.

Ultimately, if you desire to invest in real estate to earn extra cash flow and offset your taxes, then this is for you. Understand that being an active investor is like having another job. Most people are looking for a lucrative investment vehicle, not another job to add to their plate that will take up more of their time. If you're interested in speaking with me further about the benefits of being a Limited Partner or would like to move forward and invest in apartment syndications with my team and me, then scan the QR code to the right and schedule a call.

There will be investors who will struggle with the idea of giving up control even if they agree that investing passively in syndications is a great opportunity. If you ultimately feel you must be in control and are willing to sacrifice your time to be engaged in the weeds of being an active real estate investor, then being a Limited Partner may not be the best fit for you. In my experience: this is a very small group of people.

For a detailed list of all the active and passive ways you can invest in real estate, scan the QR code to obtain the checklist.

Even if your goal is to someday become an active apartment investor, investing passively as a limited partner within a few deals will help educate you about the apartment syndication process—something I like to call Syndication Pre-School or Syndication on Training Wheels. In addition, the deals you invest in can be added to your real estate resume as credibility. This is critical when speaking to brokers and lenders because you will have some experience to leverage if you did go active and pursue your own deal.

Whether you choose to be an active or passive investor, the best thing you can do is act. Not doing anything to invest in your financial future is definitely the wrong decision.

As the Nike slogan says, "Just Do It."

Chapter 7

WHAT ARE THE BENEFITS OF INVESTING AS AN LP?

I'll say this, if I could go back in time and start over in college, I would have put my first chunk of money into a real estate syndication. I could have earned passive income and accelerated my wealth early at a young age, all while still focusing on my academic studies. You all are here because something inside you wants more. You have a desire to learn how to make more money efficiently. Let's address those desires and list the numerous benefits available to those that invest in real estate syndications.

1. The ability to invest passively and leverage the expertise of the Sponsors and property management team.
2. Diversification in your investments, from typical instruments like stocks and bonds.
3. An opportunity to invest in large multifamily property deals that normally would be out of reach, and a chance to invest at a low barrier of entry.
4. Reduced risk by investing in multifamily syndications across diverse markets with various risk profiles.

5. Predictable cash flow distributions through rental income.
6. Lucrative real estate tax benefits and deductions.
7. Because a multifamily property is valued based on the income it produces, we as Operators can directly control the increase in value of the property, thus multiplying your money over the long term.
8. Legal protection of your money.
9. Playing a part in improving the quality of properties and communities for tenants and helping to transform neighborhoods.
10. More free time to use your superpowers to create impact in the world.
11. Inflation protection hedge.
12. Build your real estate resume.
13. Higher unit counts equals more stability. Unlike a single-family home, if one tenant moves out, the property will still produce cash flow and operations will not be greatly affected.
14. Forced appreciation through renovations and cutting expenses.

Chapter 8

SYNDICATION FEES & HOW SPONSORS ARE PAID

Because of all the work that Sponsors complete to get a deal under contract and execute the business plan, they are compensated through fee structures. If Sponsors did not get paid for these critical tasks, they would have to hire someone else to complete them (which would probably cost even more and dilute the profits of the deal). What's great about these GP fees is alignment of interest. Although this is not the case for every Sponsor and investment opportunity — but in principle — fees motivate the GP(s) to find and successfully operate good deals. They are not paid until certain milestones are completed.

Let's take a moment and go through a list of fees you can expect for most syndication deals:

- **Acquisition Fee**: Between 1-4% of the property purchase price. This fee is collected when Sponsors close on the deal and is proportionate to their share of the equity. This fee compensates the GP(s) for all the time-consuming underwriting and due diligence work they performed to create the investment opportunity for LP(s).

- **Refinance Fee:** Between 1-3% of the new refinanced loan. Although a refinance is not completed for every syndication deal, this fee is collected when Sponsors complete a property refinance.
- **Loan Guarantee Fee:** Usually 1% of the loan amount. This fee is collected to compensate a GP (or another high net worth individual) that personally guarantees the loan with their net worth statements or assets.
- **Asset Management Fee:** Between 1-3% of the property's gross collected income, this is a monthly or quarterly fee GP(s) are paid for the management and oversight of the property's operations such as admin tasks, investor distributions and communication, tax filing and legal paperwork, and overseeing the property management company. Having the asset management fee proportional to the income and how well the property performs creates an alignment of interest for the Sponsors to continue to perform throughout the life cycle of the deal in order to get paid. If the deal experiences a drop in income, then the GP(s) asset management fee will also dip significantly. On the other end of the spectrum, this fee can also be paid per apartment unit, with $200-$300 per unit annually being the norm. When this is the case, the fee is fixed and GP(s) are paid regardless of the deal's performance.
- **Property Management Fee:** Anywhere between 4-10% and is a percentage of the collected rent. Paid to the outside property management company that manages the property (or if management is vertically integrated, to the Sponsors. You usually see this type of structure from senior Operators and with 100+ unit deals).
- **Exit Sale/Disposition Fee:** Between 1-4% of the final sale price. This fee is collected when GP(s) exit a deal at sale and compensates them for all the work they put worth to market and sell the deal successfully.

The list above is standard metrics you should expect to see from good Operators. They can vary slightly depending on the deal itself. Be wary of syndications with high fees or GP(s) that fail to report these numbers when presenting a deal. High fee structures from GP(s) cuts into the deal's profits which ultimately means a lower return to LP investors.

Syndication Fees

ACQUISITION FEE	1 - 4 %
REFINANCE FEE	1 - 3 %
LOAN GUARANTEE FEE	1 %
ASSET MANAGEMENT FEE	1 - 3 %
PROPERTY MANAGEMENT FEE	4 - 10 %
DISPOSITION FEE	1 - 4 %

Chapter 9

WHAT IS THE PROCESS FOR INVESTING IN A LARGE APARTMENT COMPLEX?

A lot of the concepts and definitions we have discussed can seem intimidating and a lot to take in. I can imagine that the overall process of how a syndication deal is completed from start to finish might still seem hazy. Here is a timeline of what you can expect.

1. The GP(s) analyze a pre-identified market and develop solid relationships with brokers, property managers, and contractors.
2. The GP(s) underwrite and perform due diligence on multiple properties until they find one that generates enough cash flow and appreciation to offer stable and high enough yield returns to make LP investors happy.

3. The GP submits an offer and places the property under contract. Once the property is under contract, a Limited Liability Company (LLC) is formed to hold/own the property. The property is not held in the name of the GP(s). The LPs are thus investing in the property LLC itself in the form of shares. This ensures the appropriate legal protection.
4. The GP(s) take on the liabilities and manage the LLC with the property.
5. Once the property is under contract, the GP(s) will contact the LP investors (usually via email) to raise the necessary capital to fund the deal.
6. After reviewing the investment summary and or attending a webinar where the deal is discussed in further detail and questions are answered, LP(s) notify the GP(s) they are interested in investing. This is called a soft reserve/commit. It expresses your interest in investing in the deal and how much you would like to invest. It is not a legally binding commitment and does not guarantee you will have a spot in the deal.
7. *** Investing in a multifamily syndication is on a first come, first served basis. Opportunities fill up fast and are in great demand. If you are interested in investing in a deal, it is highly recommended that you review the documents and wire funds to secure your spot as soon as possible. ***
8. To successfully invest in the apartment deal and secure your spot, the LP(s) must sign and fill out two documents: The Private Placement Memorandum (PPM) & The Subscription Agreement. The PPM & Subscription Agreements are ALWAYS prepared by a licensed attorney.
9. Once the two documents are signed, investors wire their investment funds into an LLC bank account set up just for the property itself.
10. The General Partners will notify all the investors via phone call and/or email once the deal has successfully closed.
11. Every month or quarter, investors should expect to receive updates on the apartment complex from the GP(s) via email. Up-

dates will include general project timelines, renovation updates, income and expenses, market trends, occupancy rates, progress photos, etc.

Here is an example of what an email to my investors would look like:

It's been a busy month as we continue renewals ahead of the summer turnover on Mainstreet Property ABC. Check out this information and more in this month's update, which includes financials for February.

Structure of the Update:

Announcements

Key Highlights

Operations

CapEx

Market Update (if applicable)

Announcements

- □ Our lender just completed sign-off yesterday on required capex repairs and we will be receiving our capex reserves back soon.
- □ K-1s went out earlier this month. Please let us know if you could not access yours or if you have questions.
- □ Reminder that our first distribution is planned for the 6-month mark after closing.

Summary of Key Highlights

- □ We had to kick-off renewals towards the end of February and received numerous renewals at the full market rate. We have offered budgeted concessions starting about two weeks ago to try and capture a few more renewals at market that will allow us to have what we believe is a responsible turnover/new lease ratio for the summer. On new leases, we have been hitting full market values with no issues.

Operations

- □ The chart below is an overview of December's financials. The total income collected for January was $81,587.86. Rent collections for the month of February was 99.5%.
- □ Expenses are about $11k higher than normal due to our catch-up on utilities. We had to complete the fire safety portion of our capex list before the city would switch utilities to our name, but that has now been completed, so we will be billed for one month of utilities at a time moving forward.

inancials	February 2021				YTD		
	Actual	Budget	Variance		Actual	Budget	Variance
evenue							
ffective Rental Income	81,587.86	78,400.00	3,187.86		162,740.30	156,800.00	5,940.30
ther Income	875.00	500.00	375.00		2,376.25	500.00	1,876.25
ross Income	82,462.86	78,900.00	3,562.86		165,116.55	157,300.00	7,816.55
ross Operating Expenses	41,078.01	38,572.00	2,506.01		75,286.88	77,144.00	(1,857.12
et Operating Income	41,384.85	40,328.00	1,056.85		89,829.67	80,156.00	9,673.67

Capex

- □ During late February/early March, we have a full landscape job done on the premises. It's hard to appreciate the difference in the gloomy winter weather, but it was long overdue and made a tremendous difference in aesthetics.

Market Update

The Texas market continues to see lower inventory compared to last year.

"Experts say with houses selling faster, more houses are needed to meet the demand. It's estimated that Texas has 0.9 months of housing inventory compared to 2.4 months of inventory at the beginning of the year."

1. Cash flow distributions from the income the property produces will be distributed either monthly or quarterly (this can vary depending on how the deal is structured) to investors.

2. Quarterly financial reports (March, June, September, December) on the property's performance will be sent via email from the GP(s) to the LP(s). This report is way more robust than the monthly updates and will include details such as the profit and loss statements, rent rolls, and additional financial metrics.
3. Every year, each investor will receive a K1 statement that details the income, depreciation, deductions, and capital account for the investment property. You, as the investor, will give this to your CPA (real estate specific for investors), who will then use the document numbers to reduce your taxable income.
4. The hold period for most apartment syndications is between 3 to 7 years. If there is a refinance during the initial hold, investors will receive the majority if not all of their initial capital back. Once you receive your money back after the refinance, you will still continue to receive the same preferred returns (if offered).
5. When the property is sold, investors will typically receive their initial capital back in addition to their share of the profits from the equity split. Most deals fall under this category where investors will receive a big payday from the forced appreciation in the property after the hold period.
6. Yay! You just completed your first full cycle deal and are happy with the returns and the tax benefits. You are eager and ready to invest in the next multifamily syndication opportunity.

The graphic below is a summary of the investing process for Limited Partners within a multifamily syndication opportunity.

INVESTING IN A APARTMENT SYNDICATION PROCESS

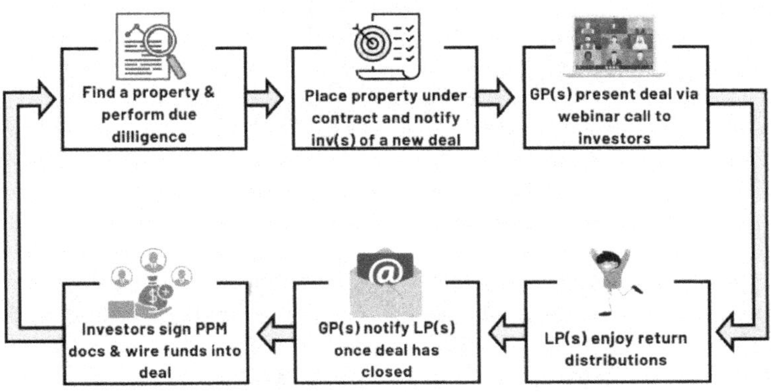

Chapter 10

HOW A DEAL IS SELECTED AND ITS LOCATION

MONDAY, 03 AUGUST 2015
LOCATION: THE MIDDLE OF NOWHERE

USS TOLEDO SSN 769 did not submerge immediately upon leaving port in Norfolk, Virginia. The water depth was too shallow. Thus, the boat stayed topside at periscope depth (PD) while it slowly navigated itself through the water channel out to the ocean. When the boat is not submerged underwater, the Officer of the Watch — a position held by a Naval Officer who is overall responsible for the safe navigation of the ship — must always be present on the bridge (the main control point where the submarine is driven).

So how in the world does the U.S. Navy dive and resurface such a formidable underwater war machine?

What allows a submarine to float and submerge underwater is the manipulation of an upward force called buoyancy. Ballast tanks throughout the submarine are filled with either water or air to alter the buoyancy of the boat and thus determine whether the submarine will submerge or sink. Once submerged — essentially a plane underwater—what allows such a gigantic metallic tube to fly through the water is by altering its sail and tail surfaces.

To go up on the bridge (when the sub is topside), you must ask permission from the Chief of the Watch (an experienced senior enlisted sailor overall responsible for controlling the sub's buoyancy, masts, and antennas).

"Chief of the Watch, permission for Evans to go up on the bridge and conduct a look about?" one of the sailors commanded.

The Chief looked at me, nodded, and said, "Very well. But, before going on the bridge, every individual must strap on a yellow harness that is used to connect him or herself to hooks so that if the boat lists or heels too hard, they do not fall overboard." I remember playing with the contraption: with all its various hooks and different buckles, putting on the harness proved to be difficult for me. It took some time before I finally received help from one of the other Officers.

I climbed up a 90-degree oriented set of wet steel stairs to get to the top of the sub that overlooked the horizon. To date, being topside on a nuclear submarine has been one of the most mesmerizing events I have ever experienced in my life. Pictures themselves cannot portray the rushing experience and mix of emotions one feels as he or she overlooks the sea riding on the top of a billion-dollar warship. Words can't explain it. You must experience it.

Even though you are traveling through the ocean, you feel like you're overlooking the entire globe. At night, the stars and the moon are clear and bright.

It was like we had our own unique location of wonder.

At that spectacular moment, with all of its splendor, I couldn't help but think about my mother and how proud she would be. I loved looking back and seeing the entire aft of the sub travel through the sea — the huge blue wake was beautiful. It made the water appear to have a rainbow of different colors. The long, slender back of the boat traveled effortlessly through the water, its tail/stern protruding from the sea. Little ebbs and flows of water rolled across the top of the aft of the sub. And if you silenced your inner thoughts and just took in the scenery, you could hear the flow of the water as it traveled around the sub and smell its salt seaweed aroma.

Everything was quiet. The sub itself. The ocean. Just quiet…

The bow of the boat moved gracefully through the vicious, yet firm grasp of the ocean waves. As the boat traveled topside within the water, the bow of the boat pierced the ocean waves in half. Dolphins swam and jumped in and out of the water, literally only a few feet in front of the bow. It aligned perfectly with the history of the nuclear submarine dolphin pin: the tale that dolphins have always been the guardians of the sea and sailors. On both the port and starboard sides, you could see beautiful rays of light rising from the surface of the water and extending across the sub.

When the submarine is on the surface, it's more limited in its ability to move. This is similar to a property. Many elements contributed to the beauty and wonder of the submarine that night. There are also numerous factors that help determine if a location is ideal or not for an investment opportunity.

Location is everything.

Some multifamily Operators prefer to focus on one or two particular markets, while others may consider various regions throughout the country. It's a common industry standard to qualify markets into three categories: primary, secondary, and tertiary.

1. **Primary (Gateway):** Major population centers (above 5 million) with various established industries and businesses such as Chicago, Los Angeles, Atlanta, San Francisco, New York, and Boston. Cap rates in primary markets are lower and more compressed than in tertiary markets due to the competition and popularity among investors.
2. **Secondary:** Markets with smaller populations (1 to 5 million) than primary but with growing commerce, jobs, and economies. They offer more affordable multifamily properties and are usually close to primary gateway cities. Examples include Austin, Dallas, San Diego, Denver, and Indianapolis.

3. **Tertiary (High-growth):** Also known as emerging markets in real estate, these smaller, more spread-out cities have a population of fewer than one million people. Tertiary markets are more suburban in nature, more affordable, have slow and steady growth in business and employment, and are less volatile during economic downturns. Examples include Charleston, Kansas City, Jacksonville, Des Moines, Colorado Springs, and Sacramento.

Location is everything for investors too.

They love investing in a property within the same geographical location as them. A certain pride comes with being able to drive or walk past a property you are a part owner in. There is also a greater comfort factor investing in a property you can visit at any time. I think back to one of the first syndication deals I did in San Diego. A lot of local people invested in the deal from excitement alone. We also even host social events at the property, such as movie nights or potlucks with drinks. Local investors love being able to show up and be a part of the experience of investing.

This is another one of the many reasons I love investing in multifamily syndications. There is a real people component that comes along with it you just don't get investing in other investment vehicles such as stocks.

There are several other important factors that General Partners consider when selecting a location to invest in. Let's review and discuss them in further detail below.

- **Population Trends:** To be a successful multifamily investor, you must also be great at understanding people. People are the number one priority in investing: both personally and from a business perspective. As Operators, one of our top missions is to meet and serve the needs of investors. A big part of understanding how to feed that need is understanding the population movement of people and their interests. We only invest in areas where population growth is increasing or has favorable uptrends. Decreasing or lackluster population movement is a negative sign we avoid.

- **Economic Diversity:** No single employer or business should dominate the market. There needs to be at least 3 strong employers or economic revenue drivers for the market you are interested in investing in. If one fails, it will not impact the employment and thus tenants' ability to pay rent (such as tourism, military, biotech, health sciences, automotive, etc.).
- **Unemployment:** Unemployment levels should be below the average percentage for the entire U.S. population. Market-specific trends should reflect that unemployment levels are either stagnant or decreasing. An increase in unemployment in a geographical area is a red flag and a sign of volatile market metrics.
- **Supply and Demand:** Analyze market trends to invest in areas where there is not a surplus of units available or under construction. An over-supply of market units will cause lower occupancy and rental income rates for an apartment complex.
- **Business & Retail Proximity:** It's no surprise that businesses and retailers such as Starbucks and Whole Foods conduct thorough research on area demographics, income and unemployment trends, and population before establishing a location there. It's smart to consider this and use this to your advantage when evaluating an area. In addition, property tenants like living within an area full of popular restaurants and retail businesses.
- **Crime:** High crime or areas showing an upward trend in crime are avoided. Although there are some rare opportunities where you can acquire a property that can be turned around to improve the surrounding community, this is usually done in gentrifying areas and among operators experienced in that type of business plan.
- **Schools:** School districts with good ratings are great indications of a strong market area. This is also a strong positive for tenants within the apartment complex because they will want their kids to attend quality schools that are safe. Again — as a multifamily investor, you have a unique opportunity to uplift and add value to communities.

- **Job Growth:** An increase in job growth in a market reflects strong economic growth. This leads to a rise in population, apartment demand, and thus rental rates.
- **Boots on the Ground:** A certain advantage comes from investing in your own backyard and being familiar with the developments or trends that are up and coming. The neighborhoods, and the properties themselves, can vary even street by street. One of the Operators must be within the same city, or no further than 3 hours away from the market we are considering investing in. That way, if we need to visit the property for emergencies or other activity concerns, we have a representative close by that can visit the property right away and address these issues. If you or none of the other General Partners live within the area, then one of you at least should still be knowledgeable about the market because you used to live or attend school there or have a network of people there that do.

Chapter 11

THE 4 TYPES OF MULTIFAMILY BUSINESS PLANS

There is a diverse spread of investment opportunities that Limited Partners can expect to see within multifamily. Each business plan is unique and will have its own expected level of risk and potential returns. When I say business plan, I am referring to — from acquisition to sale — how the property will be operated, any changes or updates that may occur, rent increases, expected expenses, debt structure and possible downsides, and the estimated hold period for the project.

These unique business plans can be categorized into four buckets: Core (or Turnkey), Core Plus, Value Add, and Opportunistic (Development). They are terms widely known in the commercial real estate sector to define the level of risk and return of the project property.

Here is what you need to know about each business plan:

1. **Core/Turnkey/Stabilized:** An apartment building with minimal upside at sale because it is still pretty new or because value has already been added (tenant occupancy of at least 95%). This style of business plan requires little work once acquired and is great for passive investors that want consistent, stable cash flow

from day 1. Maintenance is little to none and management is typically minor. The upside upon sale of the property is dependent on market appreciation.

Example: A 200-unit multifamily complex in San Antonio built in 2019 with market-rate rents and full occupancy.

2. **Core Plus:** Next to moderate or relatively low risk. Income from an apartment complex can be increased through small renovations, a change in property management, improved expenses, or better tenant selection. Similar to Core, these properties are pretty much stabilized, with minimal maintenance and capex requirements, and have a tenant occupancy of at least 85%.

Example: A 150-apartment complex in Phoenix built in 2010. There is a small opportunity to increase the property's appeal by adding a gym, dog park, Amazon lockers, changing to a new property management company, or decreasing expenses through RUBS.

3. **Value Add:** The perfect blend between market appreciation and forced appreciation. This is usually a property decently stabilized (tenant occupancy of at least 80%) with the opportunity to significantly improve the income and value of a property through renovation upgrades and decreasing operating expenses. This deal is for investors willing to take a little more risk to get a larger amount of regular cash flow and a great upside at sale.

Example: A 100- unit in Ohio built in 1985 that still has great occupancy, but needs significant repairs and capex improvements to the properties interior and exterior in order to increase rent premiums by roughly $200 (to compete with market rents of comparable properties in the area).

4. **Opportunistic/Development:** An investment opportunity where LP(s) invest in the large upside of an apartment complex being built from the ground up or an existing property/structure being redeveloped. There are usually no cash flow distributions for a while. This is a long-term play and can take several years. This type of deal is for investors that are okay with their capital being held for a significant amount of time, but are willing to take a risk to win

big on the back end when the apartment building is officially built and sold.

Example: 1970 Built 40-unit apartment building in San Diego zoned with the ability to add an additional 15 units on site.

It's important that investors understand the different business plans so they can make an informed decision about the level of risk and returns they would like to incur. The graphic below can be used as a general rule of thumb. Core has the least risk and Opportunistic, at the bottom of the pyramid, has the greatest risk (but also the highest expected reward in returns).

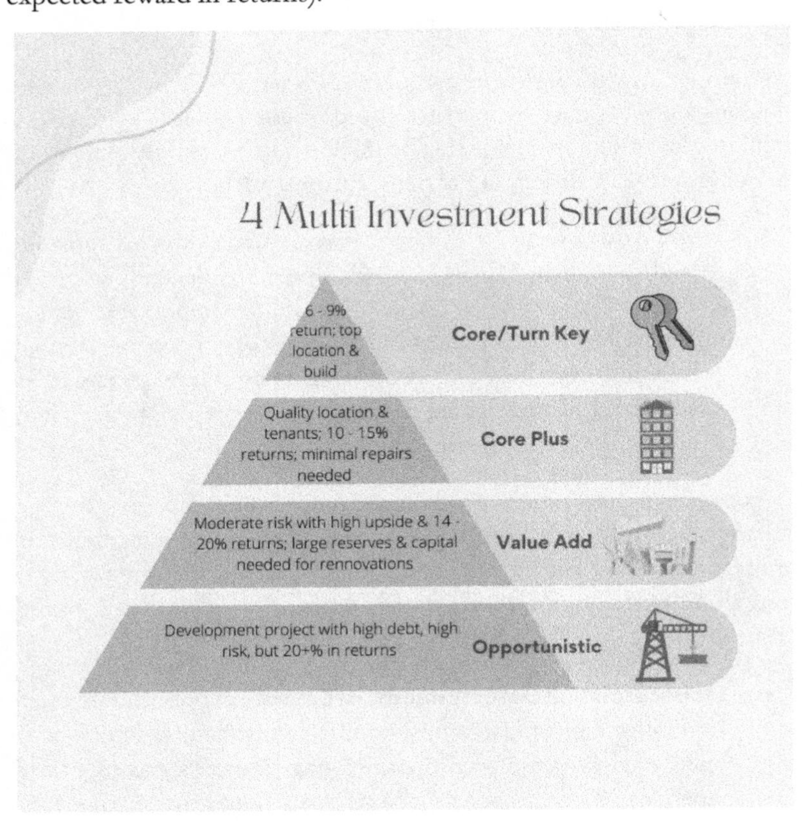

Chapter 12

WHAT TO EXPECT FROM THE WEBINAR CALL/ PRESENTATION

Multifamily syndication deals are usually presented through a conference/meeting style presentation called the Investor Webinar. This is a great opportunity for investors contemplating whether they want to invest or not, to have all their questions and or concerns addressed. This is the chance for the General Partnership to discuss all aspects of the deal, such as the investment summary, the market/ location, why they choose this deal and what makes it special, projected returns, expected challenges, and the business plan. It's also a time for Limited Partners to get to know the GP team and have their questions answered about the deal itself. I always recommend that investors attend the webinar because they'll also learn from the questions and perspective of the other investors on the call.

Most webinars are completed over Zoom, Microsoft Teams, or Google Meet. After the presentation, my team and I typically send out the recording to all of our investors to watch again on their own time.

Although it is common for Operators to host an Investor webinar, it is not required. Many deals may arise that do not offer a webinar presentation.

When I first graduated from the Naval Academy, I went back to Chicago and Newport to speak to prospective candidates and Prep School students about my experiences. Looking out at their sea of faces, I was reminded of how nervous I was before starting my training that first year. There are so many mixed emotions. Ambition. Excitement. Fear. Curiosity. Nervousness. The candidates asked me numerous questions about recommendations for success, mindset, and what life is like. I remember how humbled I felt at sharing my knowledge with them. And at that moment, a cloud of immense gratitude overtook me.

Just like speaking to candidates about the Naval Academy, the investor webinar is a similar experience because it allows you and the other Sponsors to communicate with potential Limited Partners on all aspects of the multifamily syndication opportunity.

In my experience, just sending out a pitch deck powerpoint for the deal is not enough. A lot of investors may not thoroughly understand the terms, business plan, and financial metrics. It usually requires that someone on the Sponsorship team explain everything and or answer questions. There is also a trust factor that comes from Limited Partners when they see and hear Operators speak about a deal directly themselves, instead of just receiving an email about it. It's not uncommon for investors to still call me after the webinar to speak with me personally because they were afraid to ask questions during the presentation.

I always recommend potential investors take the time to plan out a few questions they would like to ask within the webinar.

And for those that aspire to be an active syndicator one day: it's still valuable to attend a webinar so you can see how it is structured, and learn valuable insights from how the Sponsor speaks about a deal and answers investors' questions.

For a free investor webinar worksheet you can use specifically designed to take notes on during a syndication deal presentation, scan the QR code to download one.

To see what an example webinar looks like from my previous deals, contact me at drmultifamily.com

Chapter 13

WHAT IS A PRIVATE PLACEMENT MEMORANDUM (PPM)?

A PPM is a large document, between 100 to 150 pages long, that outlines everything investors need to know about the syndication opportunity and the associated risk factors. Ever since the Securities Act of 1993, it's a legal document that is required and regulated by the Security & Exchange Commission (SEC) and is prepared by an experienced securities attorney. Private placements are when shares of stock (real estate syndication shares) are issued for purchase to LP(s) under specific terms and financial criteria. It's called private because the deal is only presented or advertised to investors that meet certain criteria, not just the general public like a stock.

Whether it's stocks, cryptocurrency, bonds, or real estate—every investment has some potential risk—some more than others.

Multifamily Real Estate has proven to be one of the safest bets that offer substantial income rewards. Legally, GP(s) are required by law to still list all of the potential risk factors to investors. The private placement memorandum helps investors make the most informed decision on a syndication deal.

One critical point: often, LP investors will want to have their financial advisor or attorney review deals. There is nothing wrong with this. But just like a real estate agent and CPA, make sure your financial advisor and/or attorney specializes in working with real estate investors.

Foot stomp.

They will know what to specifically look for and offer better guidance for you.

For a checklist on how to pick a real estate attorney, scan the QR code above.

Most of the wording, down to the font size, is regulated by the Security & Exchange Commission, and is standard across PPMs you will see in other investment deals.

If you would like recommendations for CPAs or attorneys that specialize working with real estate investors, schedule a call with me and I can refer you to some (scan the QR code for the calendar link)

The exact structure of a private placement memorandum can vary from deal to deal, but in general, each PPM includes the following:

Executive Summary

Disclaimer/Investor Notices

Operating Agreement

Property Management

Fees

Company Overview & General Partnership Bios

Use of Capital Proceeds

Financial Information

Conflicts of Interest

The Offering Terms

Taxes and Legal

Investor Criteria

Risk Factors

Location of Funds

Liquidity of Funds

Timing of the Offering

Supplemental Information

How to Subscribe/Invest

Let's take a moment to dig a little deeper into each section so you all can gain a better understanding.

Executive Summary

This can have many names depending on who structures the document. This section is basically a highlight reel of all the PPM content, the property itself, and all the key points to look out for. Investors should be able to read this and have a bird's eye view of the business plan, expected return projections, market analysis, and the minimum investment amount.

Disclaimer/Investor Notices

This section begins by informing the reader that the PPM is a confidential document and cannot be distributed or reproduced in any way. It dictates that the syndication offering is exempt from registering with the SEC and explains why, that the offering is not available to the public market, that the offering has a degree of risk, transfer restrictions, and the right for investors to receive information and ask questions should they have any. The disclaimers within this section protect the syndication LLC from being investigated by the SEC and from any claims of fraud or criminal investing activity should they arise and are legally required.

Operating Agreement

This section highlights the most important items within the PPM, such as the management and operation details of the syndication, the investor waterfall/distribution hurdles, the preferred return, profit distributions at refinance or sell, the voting rights of Limited Partners, obligation requirements if a capital call were to occur, the reports General Partners will deliver to investors, Limited Partners ability at being able to transfer shares, powers of attorney, and how a member of the General Partnership could be removed.

Property Management

The section explains who will be the management company for the day-to-day operations of the syndicated property. It will list their experience and qualifications for managing the specific asset class.

Fees

This section outlines all the fees within a syndication offering that General Partners receive, such as the acquisition fee, loan guarantor fee, asset management fee, property management fee, refinance fee, and the disposition fee.

Company Overview & General Partnership Bios

This section discusses the name of the company Limited Partners are investing in that was formed to raise capital and manage the property. If the company expects to generate and distribute regular returns to investors, it will be mentioned. The biographies of each member of the General Partnerships' qualifications, education, experience, real estate track records, special skills, and their specific role to the team are included here.

Use of Capital Proceeds

Just the way it sounds, this section explains how the money raised from investors will be used throughout the acquisition and business plan of the property. Examples include renovations, reserves, capital improvements, pre-closing expenses, closing costs, down payment, earnest money deposit, fees, payroll salaries, operations, and disposition.

Financial Information

This is also a huge section within the PPM. This will discuss the historical financials, expenses, pro formas, financial risks, stress test analysis, and timeline projections.

Conflicts of Interest

This section discloses any conflicts of interest members of the General Partnership could have with investors. An example could be that the third-party property management company could also own and or manage a property next door to/down the street of the syndicated property and would thus be considered competition. Another example could be that one of the General Partners is a licensed broker that would earn a commission on closing the syndicated property.

The Offering Terms

A term sheet of all the information explained in more detail within the PPM, such as the minimum investment amount, the anticipated returns, the holding period of the property, distribution payments and schedule, and the equity structure split between the General Partnership and Limited Partners. A lot of the information here is repeated in the Executive Summary. This is also found within the Subscription Agreement.

Taxes and Legal

This section includes the documents Limited Partners can expect to receive during the hold period of the syndicated property, such as the annual K1 document and depreciation and tax implications as a Limited Partner investor. This section also discloses the history of any criminal convictions, litigations, or bankruptcies against any of the members of the General Partnership team.

Investor Criteria

This section explains the type of investors and the criteria required for them to purchase securities within the syndication. If it's a 506(b) offering, the definition and list of investors that qualify will be listed (Sophisticated). If it's a 506(c) offering, the definition and a list of investors that qualify will be listed and the process used for verifying if they are Accredited or not.

Risk Factors

The most important and longest portion of the PPM. Although syndications like multifamily are recession-resistant, it is still possible to lose money. Investors can expect to read a detailed explanation of all the potential risks involved in the syndication deal. Common risk factors discussed include natural disasters, market volatility, property management, tax challenges, tenant issues, and financing.

Location of Funds

This section explains where investors' funds are collected and held when Limited Partners transfer their capital. It also discloses what would happen to investor funds if the General Partnership failed to fully raise the necessary capital to close. Usually, funds are held within a bank account in the LLC syndication company name (typically the same name as the property itself).

Liquidity of Funds

This section clarifies to Limited Partners that their funds are not liquid once invested within the syndication offering. It is expected that their funds are held within the deal for the entire hold period. If an extreme hardship does arise where a Limited Partner would need to sell, most deals require permission from the General Partners to sell their shares.

Depending on the Sponsor, some allow Limited Partners to sell their shares while others do not. If allowed, it still requires permission from the General Partners. The sold shares could be bought by the General Partnership, sold to another Limited Partner within the group, or sold to a new Limited Partner outside the original group.

Timing of the Offering

The timeline of the syndication offering, such as the start date, when the deal would need to be canceled if the required capital was not raised, the expected date of closing if all the capital was raised successfully, and the General Partnership's rights to terminate (if risks and or red flags arise) or extend (if more time is needed to raise capital) the offering.

Supplemental Information

This section provides the contact information for the General Partnership team for investors that have questions about the syndication offering. It also includes any other further details investors may want that would be helpful to understanding the deal, such as the organizational chart of the company, appraisals, market studies, copies of leases, letters of intent, etc.

How to Subscribe/Invest

One of the final sections of the PPM that outlines the entire process of how a potential investor can subscribe to the syndication offering. This includes the required documents that need to be signed, specifying the number of shares a Limited Partner wants to purchase, how to wire and or transfer funds, and the use of the property LLC escrow or bank account.

If you have questions about the Private Placement Memorandum or about the fundamentals of syndications, book a call with me. I'd be happy to help.

Chapter 14

THE SUBSCRIPTION AGREEMENT IN ONE BITE

A subscription agreement (or partnership agreement) is a short document within the PPM. Just like the PPM, for many investors, this document can be intimidating when reviewing it for the first time due to all the legal jargon writing. It is an agreement that LP(s) will purchase shares within the LLC that holds the property at a specified price (based on how much an individual commits to invest). Basically, it's a legally binding document — regulated by the Securities and Exchange Commission (SEC) — that details the terms of an investor participating in a limited partnership.

The subscription agreements includes:

- Roles and expectations of the General Partners and Limited Partners
- Confidentiality clauses
- Limited Partner investors' shares, price, and ownership percentage
- Apartment complex LLC company information

- Limited Partner termination terms
- Method and schedule of Limited Partner distribution payments
- Voting and rights of Limited Partners within the syndication
- Financial qualifications of the Limited Partners

Usually, LP(s) can expect to receive the PPM and other syndication documents through an Investor Portal. When a deal is first offered, LP investors will be directed to a portal link that allows them to create a username and password to sign-up. From there, they can access the subscription documents and sign them electronically. GP(s) can use the portal to distribute investor earnings via ACH payments and can upload tax and other property document updates that investors can log on and view in real-time. Portals are also another way GP(s) can use to actively communicate with LP investors.

Chapter 15

WHERE TO FIND THE MONEY TO INVEST IN MULTIFAMILY

You always hear that one of the biggest factors holding people back from investing in real estate is that they do not have the money. For some of you, finding $25,000 to $50,000 to invest in an apartment syndication seems out of reach. You're not alone — there are tons of people that share this same thought process.

But what if I told you there are a variety of easy, creative ways to invest in your first syndication deal?

Below is a list of strategies:

1. **Self-Directed IRA (SDIRA):** Redirect your Roth IRA or IRA into a self-directed retirement account that can invest in real estate tax-free. If you're not sure what a self-directed IRA is, it's a tax-advantaged retirement plan that allows you to invest in other assets classes like real estate, precious metals, cryptocurrency, notes, land, oil/gas/mineral rights, tax liens, and livestock, in-

stead of just stocks and bonds. You CANNOT use a SDIRA to invest in collectibles or life insurance policies. This is an advantage for investors because it allows them to have more diversity and control over their retirement income.

You could rollover your entire existing IRA or 401(k) over into a SDIRA account.

To open a SDIRA, you must work with a SDIRA provider/custodian to set up and fund your account. Advanta IRA, uDirect, Equity Trust, Alto IRA, IRA Services Trust Company, Quest IRA, Sunwest Trust, and Rocket Dollar are some of the best self-directed companies to use to open an account with.

The standard documents you will need to set up the account are completing a General Application Form, a copy of one form of ID (driver's license or passport), a W9 social security verification form, and a copy of a statement from your current IRA or other retirement accounts. Accounts can be opened in 1 or 2 days for a transfer or initial contribution. If you're completing a rollover from a previous retirement account into a SDIRA, it can take up to 2 or 3 weeks. A separate transfer form is required for each account you move over into the SDIRA.

Once the SDIRA account is funded, you can now "direct" your money to invest in a syndication by filling out a Subscription Document form (this lists the IRA as the investor, not your personal name) and Private Purchase Direction Form. These forms give your SDIRA custodian permission to now transfer funds into the syndication deal bank account on your behalf. Other documents that may be required include the Private Placement Memorandum (PPM), the Operating Agreement, and or the estimated return projections of the deal.

You may partner funds within your SDIRA to invest in syndications. You can partner your SDIRA funds with another SDIRA, entity, or another individual person.

If partnering with another person, this typically involves forming a limited liability company (LLC) and then combining funds into a single account.

I recommend not partnering your own personal funds with a SDIRA. Some companies may allow you to complete the transaction, but this has been a constant red flag for the IRS and they will probably audit you if you do so. The IRS views this as a conflict of interest when you combine your own personal funds with the SDIRA to invest.

Distributions received from the syndication are deposited directly into the SDIRA account as cash. Individual Limited Partner gains made at the sale of the syndicated property are also deposited directly into the SDIRA account as cash, which then allows them to partake in tax-free compounded growth. Any accumulated cash distributions can invest in other multifamily syndications if the end-user desires.

*** If you need any assistance or have questions about setting up a SDIRA, please contact me at drmultifamily.com ***

2. **TSP (Thrift Savings Plan):** The retirement account for Government Employees & Veterans. You can take a personal loan out against your TSP (which you pay back to yourself at a low interest rate) and use that to invest in syndications.

   For more information about the TSP loan and to speak with a representative visit their website at tsp.gov.

3. **Stocks:** Proceeds from selling shares.
4. **401(k):** Roll over your 401(k) into a self-directed IRA to use to invest in apartment syndications, establish a solo 401(k), take out a loan from your 401(k), or use money from an existing 401(k) at work.

   A Solo 401(k) is also known as a self-directed 401(k), which is used by small businesses or those that are self-employed.

   Many people don't realize that you can use the funds from an old employer 401(k) to invest in multifamily syndications. You can work with your old employer's plan administrator to transfer your funds into a solo 401(k) or Self-Directed IRA.

   As of this writing, you can take out a loan on your 401(k) up to $50,000 or 50% of your total retirement account (whichever is less) within a 12-month period. The interest you pay on the loan is paid back into your own retirement account, so essentially, you are borrowing and paying yourself back (similar to the TSP loan for the government and military). Usually, the interest is a low rate as well and less than what you would see from a regular bank loan. The only fee you pay is a small loan origination or admin fee. There is no lender or credit history involved either to take out the loan, and you can usually receive your funds fast (within a matter of days).

5. **Refinance/Sale of Home:** Use the money obtained from refinancing or selling your home.
6. **Home Equity Loan or Home Equity Line of Credit (HELOC):** For most Americans, the vast majority of their net worth is held up in untapped equity within their primary residence. But what if I told you you could use the equity in your home as a loan to invest?

   With a home equity loan, you can borrow against the equity in your home as a second mortgage. You receive your money as a lump sum and banks usually offer very competitive rates because the loan is secured against using your home as collateral. The loan term can range from 5 to 30 years and banks typically lend up to 80% of the property value. Just like when you first bought your property, using a home equity loan will require you to pay closing costs, unfortunately.

   On the other hand, a HELOC is a line of credit loan that uses the equity in your property as collateral. Interest rates are usually variable, but there is a fixed-rate HELOC option as well. Borrowers can typically take up to 85% of the equity in their homes. Because a HELOC is a credit line, funds are usually accessed via a checkbook or a credit card provided to you by the bank.

   If the value of your property continues to rise, you have the option to take out multiple HELOCs or home equity loans.
7. **Liquid Cash:** Capital within a Checking or Savings Account.
8. **Other Items:** Cash from selling items you own, such as boats, luxury vehicles, collectible art, antiques, timeshares, etc.

9. **Life Insurance:** Most people don't realize the power of a whole life insurance policy. One of its best-kept secrets is your ability to borrow against the equity in your life insurance policy to invest (infinite banking).

   That doesn't mean you can just open an account today and you'll have money to use to invest with. The account needs to be open for a period of years before there is significant equity you can tap into and leverage. What's also great about this strategy is that taking a loan against your whole life insurance policy does not require a credit check, interest rates are usually lower than traditional loans, withdrawals are tax-free, and you continue to build cash value in the policy even while borrowing.

   The secret of leveraging your life insurance policy as an investment vehicle was discovered by a man named Nelson Nash (who is known as the father of the infinite banking concept). For more information on the infinite banking concept, check out Nelson Nash's book, *Becoming Your Own Banker.*

10. **Partner up with 2 or 3 Buddies and Invest Through an LLC:** Pull money together among two or more people and use that to invest in a deal. Create a single LLC where all the individuals joining to invest are listed as members. For example, two friends might come together and each commit $25,000 to invest $50,000 into a syndication opportunity.

11. **Health Savings Account (HSA):** Although the upfront purpose of an HSA account is for people to save up for medical expenses in the future, many also use them to save additional income for retirement. Some employers offer HSA plans to their employees (which is transferable if you change employers). Every contribution you make reduces your taxable income (meaning you pay less in income taxes), withdrawals are tax-free, and the money within your account grows tax-free, making HSAs a better tax-advantaged retirement vehicle than traditional IRA or 401(k) retirement accounts.

    But that's the smallest benefit. There's another option that many people don't know about.

You can use your HSA to invest in a real estate syndication through a self-directed HSA.

What's astonishing is that roughly 4% of the HSA accounts nationwide are actually used to invest with.

The result?

Thousands of untapped money left on the table that can be used as leverage to invest in lucrative, income-producing opportunities like apartment syndications.

The process for transferring your HSA account into a self-directed HSA is very similar to setting up a standard self-directed IRA, as described earlier (see bullet point #1).

Investors have two options to pick from when establishing a self-directed HSA. They can either have a Custodian Controlled Account or Checkbook Account. A Custodian Controlled Account means that a designated custodian directly controls the transfer and use of the funds within the account from the HSA owner. An investor does not have direct control on withdrawing funds. On the other hand, a Checkbook Controlled Account is when an investor opens an LLC Business Checking Account (where the HSA funds will be held) and uses the funds from there to invest in a syndication.

Investors can use their self-directed HSA to pool their money together and partner with other investors (SDIRA, HSA, individual funds) or with their own personal self-directed retirement plan to invest in a syndication offering. Another bonus benefit is that you can open more than one HSA account.

As of 2022, the annual contribution limit into an HSA is $3,650 for individuals, $7,300 for family plans, $4,650 for individuals 55 and older, and $8,300 for family plans age 55 and older. It's smart to use your HSA to invest in a real estate syndication because it allows an investor to accelerate the growth instead of being confined to the limited annual contribution amounts.

12. **Education Savings Account (ESA):** Also known as the Coverdell Savings Account. A standard education savings account is used by individuals to cover education expenses such as tuition,

book, school supplies, tutoring, room and board, etc. However, you can also create a Coverdell Self-Directed ESA that can be invested in apartment syndications.

Just like the standard SDIRA and self-directed HSA, self-directed ESAs can be set up to have checkbook control or have funds managed by a custodian.

IRA Financial or Advanta IRA specialize in setting up self-directed ESAs and are my recommended references.

As of 2021, the annual contribution limit into an ESA is $2,000.

13. **Underperforming Real Estate Assets such as land or residential property that is producing low returns or has a lot of issues**: Multifamily real estate has historically provided the highest risk-adjusted returns compared to every other real estate asset class.

14. **1031 Drop & Swap:** A drop and swap is seen among real estate deals with multiple investors (such as syndications) that allows for numerous exit strategies. Upon the sale of a multifamily property, investors can 1031 exchange their investment into the next deal with the same sponsor. This allows investors to defer the taxes they would have to pay on the gain.

    You just have to use the same entity that owned the property to be the same entity purchasing the new property. There also has to be the same number of investors in each deal (but they don't have to be the same people). You can swap out different people as long as the number of investors is the same.

    Let's say you had a syndication of 35 investors in a property called THE RETREAT. As standard, the limited liability company created to hold the property will be its name and is titled THE RETREAT LLC. At the end of a hold period of 5 years, the GP(s) decide to sell. Current investors within the syndication have the option to leave but would have to pay capital gains on any profits they earned from sale. Their positions would be bought out and swapped with new, different investors.

The 1031 Drop & Swap process is a lot easier than the TIC structure.

15. **1031 Exchange funds from sale into a syndication using Tenants In Common (TIC):** Essentially, you are doing a Joint Venture with the GP(s) to gain ownership and invest within the apartment syndication. The 1031 investor must co-own and be on the direct deed of the property and will thus be required by the lender to complete the underwriting process such as a credit check, financial statements, and a business/real estate resume. When a Limited Partner normally invests in multifamily syndication, they are buying a percentage of ownership shares within the property. This is considered a security exchange in the eyes of the IRS. The IRS has specific rules that investors must adhere to to qualify for the tax-deferred advantages of a 1031 exchange. The biggest factor is the exchange of a "like-kind" property. Using 1031 funds to directly invest in multifamily syndication would be considered an exchange of real property into securities, not an exchange of real property into another real property.

    When the syndicated property is eventually sold, a TIC structure gives an investor the option to roll those funds into another syndication or a different real estate investment opportunity.

16. **Self-Directed Simplified Employee Pension (SEP) IRA:** Essentially, this is a retirement plan for small businesses. Even if you yourself are an entrepreneur, but plan to hire employees in the future, the SEP IRA allows the business owners to later fund employee retirements. That's the biggest difference between the SEP IRA and a solo 401(k). With a solo 401(k) plan, it only covers you as the business owner and or your spouse. In addition, a solo 401(k) is more expensive and complex to set up compared to the SEP IRA.

Aside from the difference in employees, a self-directed SEP IRA has very similar metrics to the solo 401(k). Both allow entrepreneurs to invest in multifamily and syndications, in addition to other investment asset classes.

Chapter 16

HOW DO I GET PAID IN A SYNDICATION DEAL & WHEN?

THE PREF

The return metrics and structure of a syndication can vary by deal. However, below is what you will commonly see.

The Limited Partners receive a Pref or preferred return, which is paid to them either monthly or quarterly. A preferred return means that as an LP investor, you are paid first before the GP(s) receive any income from cash flow or sale proceeds. A typical preferred return is between 6–10%, with the most common being about 8%.

Put simply: that means the entire 8% will go to you FIRST before GP(s) receive a single dime. This makes the interests of the LP(s) a priority and forces the GP(s) to operate the deal to perform to a minimum standard for them to get paid. Multifamily syndications with a more limited upside at sale of the property or that are higher risk as an investment will usually pay a higher preferred return. The LP(s) receive all of the cash flow from the deal until their preferred return is reached.

If income is low for a quarter or the first few years (due to underperformance or renovations), it's common for the preferred return to accumulate over time until it is caught-up to pay LP investors their promised return at either the sale of the property, or during the life of the business plan for the project. LP(s) will find comfort in this concept knowing that GP(s) will not be paid when a deal is underperforming. Most income distributions are paid to LP(s), usually a few months after the GP(s) close on the apartment complex. Distribution payments are directly deposited into the LP investors' bank accounts.

For example, let's say that LP(s) are supposed to receive a 9% pref. During the first year of operations, the apartment complex returned a 4% pref instead. Thus, in order to "catch up" to provide investors their projected 9% preferred return on average, they should receive a higher 14% pref in year two.

Although this is the norm today, it's important to note that not every syndication will pay a preferred return. A good, strong deal might pay no pref at all. Not every deal will have a catch up either. The deal could be structured where if the projected preferred return is not met, any further returns would be neglected and considered null. I'd be cautious of deals that do not have a catch up option for Limited Partners in achieving their preferred return.

EQUITY SPLIT

Once LP investors receive their preferred returns, profits are split between the LPs and GP(s) (this is called the Equity Split or Promote). A common split is 70/30 or 80/20—where 70% goes to the LP(s) and 30% to the GP(s). This split only happens AFTER the Limited Partners receive their preferred return. This type of structure, where the Limited Partners receive a certain profit split after their preferred return hurdle is reached, is called a waterfall (more on this later). Remember: preferred returns are not guaranteed in every deal. Some syndications might be structured where profits are split straight 70/30 or 80/20.

The structure of multifamily syndication deals can vary widely and there are pros and cons to each model structure.

Don't get hung up on the numbers: A 90/10 split is not necessarily a better deal than a 75/25 split. Consider all the financial return metrics within an apartment syndication deal. A 90/10 split might give more equity to LP(s) and sound more enticing, but the overall cash-on-cash return might be lower compared to a 75/25 split.

HURDLES & WATERFALLS

Hurdles allow the General Partners to gain a larger percentage of the equity split after they have been able to achieve the projected benchmark returns to Limited Partners. This, again, is a way to incentivize and motivate the GP(s) to over perform on the deal.

For example, a hurdle might be that the equity split is 80/20 until a 16% IRR is reached. Once the Limited Partners receive 16%, any returns above that would be split 50/50.

This is a simple scenario, but it can get more complicated — which is where waterfalls come into play.

We all know what physical waterfalls are. It's a point where a river or stream of water flows over a ledge or a series of step drops" into a larger body of water. Think of syndication waterfall structures in this same way. The overall cash flow returns is the water itself, and the hurdle rates are the ledge or step drops.

General Partners need to operate the deal to achieve a certain profit to move to each hurdle. It's like a cause and effect.

Let's consider another example. Here's how a more detailed waterfall would look.

- LP(s) are supposed to receive an 8% pref with a 14% IRR. After the pref is distributed, profits between LP(s) and GP(s) are split 80/20 until the deal reaches a 14% IRR (overall return).
- Equity split of 70/30 once LP(s) achieve an IRR return of 17%
- Equity split of 60/40 once LP(s) achieve an IRR return of 19%
- Equity split of 50/50 for any IRR returns above 19%

As you can see, waterfall structures are deal specific and can get complicated. But it aligns the interests of the GP(s) and LP(s) and is a win-win for both parties. General Partners are rewarded for achieving higher and higher returns. Limited Partners favor waterfall structures because even though the equity split continues to get smaller and smaller, it's a result of the deal continuing to achieve higher returns.

Chapter 17

UNDERSTANDING DEBT AND THE CAPITAL STACK

The capital stack is the total money involved in the purchase of a real estate investment property. The reason it's called a stack is because — just like Crayola crayons — money in real estate is categorized in different colors based on who receives priority on being paid first. A typical stack has something called Senior Debt (primary loan to acquire the asset) at the bottom, then Mezzanine Debt (which is optional), then Preferred Equity (also optional), then Common Equity (also Sponsor Equity for GP(s)) at the very top. The positions at the top of the capital stack are a higher risk, but also could experience higher returns. Preferred equity is very similar to the preferred securities we see in the stock market world. Its purpose is to provide LP investors with flexible return options. For GP(s), preferred equity makes it easier to raise capital for a deal, particularly among private equity groups and institutional investors.

Senior debt is the traditional debt most of us think of when we work with a lender to buy a home. For multifamily, we would typically expect the lender to finance 70% to 80% of the property value. Second position on the stack and subordinate to Senior debt is Mezzanine debt. This debt is usually extended by private lenders or seller financing. The equity portion of the stack refers to the cash needed to close the deal, which can come from either yourself, partners, or investors. Below is a visual representation of the capital stack and the associated risk and return depend on what level you're at.

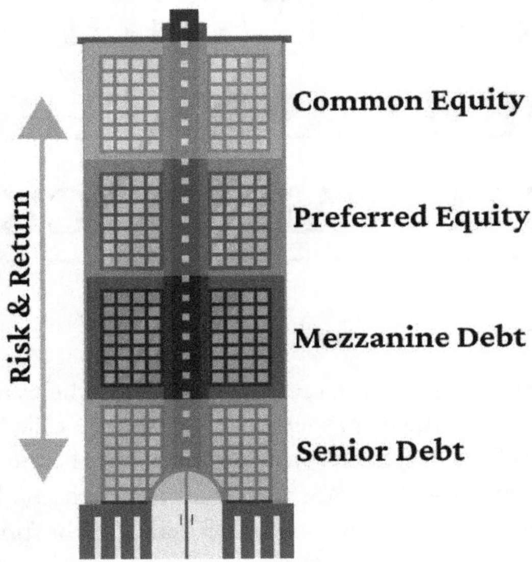

THE SINGLE-TIER STACK

In a typical, simplified syndication structure, Common equity would be split into Class A and Class B shares, with Class A consisting of Limited Partners and Class B for General Partners. When a property is sold at disposition, the senior debt is paid back first, then LP investors in Class A shares receive their initial capital back. Next, there is the common equity split of 70/30 and 80/20, as we mentioned briefly above, with 70% of the profits at sale going to LP(s) and 30% going to GP(s).

Now, this is where things can get a little bit more complicated. Hang in there with me for this one.

THE DUAL-TIER EQUITY STACK

In this structure, like in the single-tier stack above, we start with senior debt: the primary loan used to acquire and finance the investment property. The bank gets paid first.

Next, depending on the deal, preferred equity can be further divided into two classes: Class A and Class B (sometimes called Series A or Series B as well). Think of the LP group being split into: a cash group and a value group. Again: not every syndication deal will have this split equity structure for Limited Partners to choose from, but lately, it has become more popular among syndication deal opportunities.

Class A has a higher priority than Class B on the capital stack, which means they get paid first in the equity section of the stack. Once all lenders (senior debt and mezzanine debt) are paid on the capital stack, that's when owners of preferred equity receive their stable, secure distribution payments.

LP(s) may like preferred equity Class A shares because the returns are consistent at a fixed rate with also a higher preferred return (like a 10% pref). This is kind of like a loan. The Class A preferred equity position is the closest Limited Partners can get to a guaranteed return within a syndication deal (downside protection). This is the cash group.

Something drastic where the deal goes completely off the rails would need to happen for Class A investors to not receive their distributions. If Class A investors are not paid, that means no one else gets paid. In addition, depending on how the syndication is structured, preferred equity share investors may have a right to seize ownership of the property if there was a default in payment. This serves as a significant hedge against risk for LP investors.

The upside to this is that even if a deal underperforms, preferred equity investors experience less risk due to the higher returns paid out to them sooner than the other LP investors who hold a stake in Class B.

However, there is a downside. Investors with Class A shares do not participate in the upside of the deal at sale like Class B investors do. Once Class A investors get their higher preferred return, that's it (meaning, they do not participate in the 70/30 or 80/20 split at the end). On the back end, if the deal performs well, preferred equity Class A investors could receive lower returns than Class B investors.

Class B investors receive no money until Class A investors' required returns are met. There is much more risk for Class B investors, but the potential to have a higher total annualized return is greater. This is the value group.

Deals with a dual-class equity structure give LP(s) different return options to choose from. It's critical that investors pick the correct equity class that aligns with their investor needs, risk levels, and or interests.

If you would like help with determining what capital stack structure is best for you, your family, and your investment goals, schedule a free discovery call with me by scanning the QR code.

Chapter 18

THERE ARE TWO INVESTOR CATEGORIES IN A SYNDICATION

When investing in a syndication, investors are labeled by the Securities and Exchange Commission (SEC) as either Accredited or Sophisticated. To be considered an **Accredited Investor**, you must meet one the following criteria:

1. Have an income of at least $200,000 (or $300,000 jointly with a spouse) within the last two years.
2. Have a minimum net worth of $1 million, either individually or jointly with a spouse. This net worth excludes the value of your primary residence.

    Roughly 8.5% of the U.S population qualifies as accredited investors. The Securities and Exchange Commission (SEC) established these criteria because they believe that, due to the Accredited Investors high net worth or financial success, they can assume more investment risk if their money is lost in a sophisticated deal offering. By default, in the eyes of the SEC, they are considered seasoned investors. To verify the status of an individual as Accredited or not, most Sponsors use an outside third-party verification service or platform.

Syndication deals will normally be classified as either 506(b) or 506(c) offerings. Only Accredited Investors can participate within a 506(c) deal. Sponsors can publicly advertise and promote the deal on billboards, social media, across the internet, podcasts, air balloons, or whatever medium they choose to. This is a big upside for Accredited Investors because it allows them to participate in a more diverse pool of syndication deal opportunities.

A **Sophisticated Investor** is a nonaccredited investor with the ability to make an educated decision: whether investing in a multifamily syndication is a good option for them or not. Put simply, a sophisticated investor is everyone that is not accredited. You do not have to have a certain net worth or knowledge about real estate.

Sophisticated Investors can partake in 506(b) syndication deals only. Over 80% of apartment syndications will utilize a 506(b) offering. The biggest downside to the 506(b) is that it only allows for thirty-five non-accredited investors and an unlimited number of spots for Accredited Investors. 506(b) Deals cannot be publicly advertised.

Chapter 19

THE RETURN METRICS IN AN APARTMENT SYNDICATION

This is one of the most important things passive investors want to hear about — and rightfully so — so let's talk about it. Most syndications will pay a cash-on-cash return of 8–12% annually, an internal rate of return (IRR) of 16-24%, and an equity multiple of 1.8x–2.5x, and an average annual return of 17-25%.

Cash-on-Cash Return (CoC): The annual return you receive on your money based on the initial investment amount (expressed as a percentage).

$$CoC = \frac{Cash\ Flow\ (Annual)}{Initial\ investment}$$

Internal Rate of Return (IRR): The time rate of return of your money. This is a metric that confuses many. IRR considers the time value of money, the regular cash flow distributions you receive, and the returns you receive at the refinance or sale of the property. Thus, the IRR, in a way, represents the overall return you would receive. Essentially, you as an investor want your money back as quickly as possible. The faster you receive your initial capital back, the happier you are because you now have the freedom to use that money again for whatever you please. The faster you receive your money back from the deal, the higher the IRR; the longer your money is within the investment deal, the lower the IRR (3 years compared to 7). To keep it simple, $50,000 today will be worth more than $50,000 years from now. When comparing an apartment syndication to other investment vehicles (such as stocks or bonds), the IRR is the return metric you use, not cash-on-cash return.

Equity Multiple: A metric that essentially indicates how much your money will grow over a period of years. I love explaining this to investors because it's easy for them to grasp and understand right away, vice trying to show them other more complicated return metrics such as IRR and waterfall distributions. For example, an equity multiple of 1.0x means you broke even — if you invested $50,000 into a deal, you would receive $50,000 back. An equity multiple greater than 1.0x means you will make more money back than what you initially invested. For example, an equity multiple of 2.0x means you doubled your money—if you invested $50,000 into a deal, you would receive $100,000 back. An equity multiple less than 1.0 means you lost money. An equity multiple of 3.25x means that for every $1 invested, your money has grown/you will receive $3.25.

$$Equity\ Multiple = \frac{Total\ Profit}{Total\ Cash\ Invested}$$

If you invested $50,000 into a syndication and received $41,000 in cash distributions, then your equity multiple would be 1.82 ($50,000+ $41,000/$50,000).

Another great thing about the equity multiple is that it can be used to quickly determine the annual rate of return. The formula is:

$$\textit{Annual Rate of Return} = \frac{\textit{Equity Multiple} - 1}{\textit{Period of Years}}$$

Consider this example, say you invest in a multifamily syndication that produces an equity multiple of 2.2 over 5 years. That would mean it has an annual rate of return of 24% [(2.2-1)/5].

Average Annual Return (AAR): A metric that indicates the average annual return over a set amount of years for a multifamily property. It is determined by taking the total earnings from a property (regular cash flow distributions plus the profits at sale) and dividing that by the initial investment amount. That number is then divided by the total hold period of the project in years.

$$\textit{Avg Annual Return} = \left(\frac{\textit{Total Earnings (cashflow + profits at sale}}{\textit{Initial Investment Amount}}\right) \textit{(Hold Period in Years)}$$

For example, if you invested $100,000 into a syndication and received a total of $32,000 in cash flow earnings and another $68,000 in profits at sale in year 4, that would equate to an average annual return of 25%.

Chapter 20

OTHER IMPORTANT METRICS YOU MUST KNOW ABOUT

Capitalization Rates (or cap rate for short): The good ol' cap rate. This metric is one of the most frequently discussed terms in the commercial real estate arena. Ironically, they offer little value in analyzing multifamily properties because of how easily the percentage can be manipulated. Cap rates are the percentage return an inventory would receive on a property if they paid all cash for it. Cap rates are used to calculate what a property is worth by considering its Net Operating Income (NOI).

$$Cap\ Rate\ (\%) = \frac{NOI}{Property\ Value}$$

Cap rates are inversely proportional to purchase price and market value of the property. A low cap rate represents a high purchase price (such as markets like California or Texas), while a high cap rate indicates a lower purchase price (Ohio or Michigan). This also includes risk. Investment properties with low cap rates are considered more stable and with lower risk.

For example, a 7-unit apartment complex in Los Angeles with a purchase price of $2,399,000 and a NOI of $77,537, would have an estimated cap rate of 3.24%.

($77,537/$2,399,000) = 0.032 * 100% = 3.24%

Now compare this with a 71-unit apartment complex in Alabama with a purchase price of $3,100,000 and a NOI of $180,245. This would yield an estimated cap rate of 5.81%.

($180,245/$3,100,000) = 0.0581*100 = 5.81%

What if I asked you if the NOI we used was based on the current trailing three-month revenue instead of the trailing twelve-month financials? What about are occupancy rates for the property unusually high or low? Was there a spike in expenses one month due to a necessary capex or repair? These questions would greatly affect the NOI of the property, and drastically alter the cap rates. It's questions like these that make cap rates an ambiguous metric to take seriously when analyzing an apartment complex. They should be used holistically as a benchmark, along other metrics and factors, to determine the overall performance of a property. To add to this, Brokers and sellers will advertise the cap rate to be higher (which indicates a better deal) to excite buyers. Instead, we like to look at the trends of multiple cap rates for a market we are interested in.

Net Operating Income (NOI): The difference between the **Gross Income** (the total income the property produces, such as rent, laundry, parking, pet fees, applications fees, storage, etc.) minus the **Operating Expenses** (items that are a MUST for the property to function on a day-to-day basis, such as property management, maintenance and repairs, insurance, property taxes, landscaping, etc.). The debt service is not included in the expenses.

$$NOI = Gross\ Annual\ Income - Total\ Operating\ Expenses$$

As you can see, NOI has a direct correlation in its ability to control the value of a property. The higher the NOI (or income), the more the property is worth. The following are multiple ways an apartment complex can produce income:

- Unit Rent
- Parking (covered or extra space)
- Application Fees
- Late Fees
- Cable or Internet Bundle Packages
- Laundry
- Pet fees
- Vending machines
- Storage Units
- Tenant Utility Reimbursement
- Flat-Rate Utility Tenant Fee
- Trash pick-up

Gross Rent Multiplier (GRM): A metric that quickly determines the value of a property and estimates how many years it would take to pay off the debt service with the rental income the property produces. It's also a great metric to use to compare the difference in income between various properties in a similar market.

$$GRM = \frac{Purchase\ Price}{Gross\ Rental\ Income}$$

A good GRM will range between 7-12. For expensive markets with low cap rates, a good GRM would range between 13-19.

For example, let's say there is a property with a purchase price of $3,000,000 and a gross potential income of $380,000. The resulting GRM would be:

$3,000,000/$380,000 = 7.89

Upon further analysis, we determined that most of the other properties in the area had a GRM of 9. Because the example property with a

GRM of 7.89 is lower compared to what the average is for the market, that is a positive sign and an indicator of a good potential investment.

Let's take this a step further and use the GRM equation to estimate the potential value of a property.

Let's assume an apartment complex produces $150,000 in gross income and an average market GRM of 8. The estimated value of the multifamily would be:

$$GRM \times \text{Gross Potential Income} = \text{Property Value}$$

8 x $150,000 = $1,200,000

Last, if you know the average GRM for the properties within the market area and the purchase price, you can estimate what the potential income is for the property. This is valuable as a metric because income is not always listed when evaluating a specific property.

$$\frac{\text{Purchase Price}}{GRM} = \text{Rental Income}$$

If a property is valued at $2,000,000 and has an average area GRM of 7, then the estimated rental income produced from the property would be:

$$\frac{\$2{,}000{,}000}{7} = \$285{,}714$$

After further analysis, if you found out that the rental income the property actually produced was greater than $285,714, then that is a strong case the property could be a good investment opportunity worth pursuing. On the other end, if the actual income is less than $285,714, this indicates the property is producing less income compared to other apartments in the market area.

Debt Service Coverage Ratio (DSCR): A ratio that is a measure of how much cash is available to pay the debt on a given property. A

DSCR of 1.0 means that the property produces enough income to satisfy paying off 100% of the debt. Most lenders require a ratio of at least 1.25. When we underwrite a deal, a property has to achieve a DSCR of 1.25 or higher.

$$\text{DSCR} = \frac{\textit{Net Operating Income (NOI)}}{\textit{Total Debt Service}}$$

Chapter 21

WHAT ABOUT THE TAX BENEFITS FOR INVESTING?

Disclaimer: I am not a CPA or an attorney. The information below is a top-level view of the tax benefits. If you wish to consult with a CPA or an attorney, make SURE they specialize in working with real estate investors—this is critical.

For a checklist on what to look for in a real estate investor CPA, scan the QR code.

When you invest as a Limited Partner, the loan interest, depreciation (which is an income tax deduction), and property taxes from the investment property are passed down to you. At the end of the year in March, LP(s) will receive a Schedule K-1 statement from the GP(s).

The beauty of real estate is that even in most cases where the apartment syndication has continued to produce positive income, the K-1 statement will show a paper loss due to the write-offs from the interest, depreciation, and property taxes. This is why we all love real estate. It allows you to offset your W2 income and pay little to no taxes while still receiving positive cash flow from the income a property produces. This same concept applies to investing in an apartment syndication. Regardless of the income received in cash flow from the property, the taxable gain each year will usually be negative (or close to negative). The average loss on a K-1 statement is about $8k on a $100k Limited Partner investment.

The number values on a K-1 are generated by completing a tax deferral strategy known as a cost segregation study. A team of tax advisors and qualified engineers are hired to dissect and calculate the lifecycle of the building's construction costs, exterior and interior components, and non-structural items. They then accelerate the depreciation over 27.5 years (the lifecycle of multifamily properties) and condense it down to one year (39 years for nonresidential commercial real estate). This is known as bonus depreciation. This front-loads every depreciation deduction on the multifamily property so GP(s) can increase cash flow and defer federal and state income taxes. It's a strategy that allows the members of a syndication deal to pay little to no taxes. Basically, every component (such as carpeting, plumbing fixtures, wiring, electrical outlets, fencing, parking lots, flooring, cabinetry, appliances, countertops, etc.) of the building has a tax lifespan according to the IRS (usually 5, 10, and 15 years, depending on the component).

Although the cost can vary depending on the firm, a typical cost segregation study is between $10,000 to $25,000 and takes 30 to 60 days to complete.

One last point on legal/taxes: when you invest in a syndication, there are no tax or legal differences from investing in your individual name or an LLC you created because the apartment complex itself is already held in a single LLC.

Chapter 22

THE REAL TRUTH ABOUT FINANCIAL ADVISORS

Now more than ever, we are in a financial education crisis. Investors are bombarded with a rainbow of various investment opportunities, and it can be stressful and overwhelming on what to select. Naturally, we turn to seek guidance from those we perceive are the experts for advice — our financial advisors. This section is not meant to criticize financial advisors or imply they are bad people.

They are not.

But even with the best intentions, many financial advisors are incentivized to push their clients to invest in certain funds or opportunities they as advisors profit from. It was important for me to address this because I have had quite a few investors who were instructed by their financial advisors to not invest in syndications or real estate, who later came back wanting to invest in our deals. They regretted listening to their advisors. The job of your financial advisor is to provide the full scope of all the risks associated with all investment opportunities. Which, if done correctly, would eliminate funds and stocks altogether and make real estate the number one choice.

Just like your CPA and attorney, make sure your advisor understands real estate and is an investor themselves. That way, they can offer you true, thorough guidance on how to select the right real estate opportunities.

I cannot stress this enough. This seems to be a topic few people want to talk about or address head-on. But I want to be straight up with you all about all matters concerning real estate investments.

Chapter 23

UNDERSTANDING THE K-1 STATEMENT

The Schedule K-1 is a document that the GP partnership uses to report the income earnings, deductions, credits, and losses for each individual LP investor. K-1 statements are prepared using IRS form 1065, which is issued to any business that operates as a partnership (such as a syndication). A separate K-1 statement will be issued for each syndication an LP invests in.

You have heard me talk briefly about the K-1 statement before. But now let's dig deeper and walk through the common line items and boxes on the K-1 that investors should pay attention to:

- **LINE 2 - Net Rental Real Estate Income (loss):** Based on the LP(s) share of ownership in the deal, this is how much money they made or lost. This is the number you use to offset your taxable income, which sometimes could be as low as $0. Just because you have a negative number here does not mean that property is not performing well due to a loss of income or capital. It is negative because of the accelerated depreciation applied to the property. A negative net loss means the overall depreciation calculated for the property exceeded the net income it produced. This is a good thing. Line 2 is calculated by subtracting the net revenue minus expenses minus all depreciation.

- **LINE 19 - Distributions:** This is the total cash distributions you received for the year as an investor. Distributions come from the Net Operating Income (NOI) the property produces.

  K1 distributions are not taxed.

- **Box G:** This box reports the Limited Partners ownership percentage.

- **Box L:** The Capital Account or tax basis for the LP, not the actual account balance of capital for the property. No matter what the ending balance is for this section, it will not change or affect the preferred return/distributions that a Limited Partner receives. It shows how much an LP originally invested at the start of the deal, any additional contributions, the distributions they received, and the ending capital balance.

  The "Beginning Capital Account" is how much the LP invested from the beginning (usually $50k to $100k)

  The "Current Year Increase/Decrease" is the paper loss the property produced for the year (LINE 2)

  "Withdrawals & Distributions" is LINE 19

  The 'Ending Capital Account" shows investors what their capital gains tax situation will look like. If an LP sold his or her shares of the investment ownership, the "Ending Capital Account" balance would be subtracted from the sale proceeds to calculate what the capital gains tax will be at sale. If this number is negative, it is added to the total sales proceeds.

For an example K-1 statement, scan the following QR code.

Chapter 24

WHAT ARE THE RISKS WITH INVESTING IN MULTIFAMILY SYNDICATION?

"Valiant Warrior. 3 souls. Fuel state 1+40. You have green deck for landing," I commanded on the comms. I was the Helicopter Control Officer (HCO) on board the guided-missile defense Destroyer USS JOHN FINN DDG-113. It was like being an air traffic controller, but more up close and personnel.

It was a high-stakes, stressful job. I always had to be on high alert for anything that looked out of place. I also had to look out for the safety of the aircraft and the pilot's landing, as well as the sailors on the flight deck. Sometimes, I had to pay attention to all of this WHILE the warship rocked back and forth heavily out at sea!

It was extremely dangerous.

"Roger, Valiant Warrior inbound," the pilot radioed back.

The U.S Navy MH-60R helicopter made a slow descent to the ship. The tower was attached to the back of the ship, but it was so close to the flight deck that when a helo landed, its rotor blades were only a few feet from the very glass I looked out of.

One particular day, one of the helicopter pilots made a mistake that almost crashed the back end of the tail rotor on the deck, which would have killed all my sailors and potentially the pilot's.

My flight deck sailors were on the helo pad, waiting to chalk and chain the aircraft the moment it touched down. Chalk and chain is when you place large yellow blocks around the wheels of the helicopter to keep them in place from moving, and then chains are applied to the aircraft and attached to the helo deck. This is a necessary safety precaution to prevent the aircraft from tipping over if the ship were to experience a large roll out at sea.

Chak-chak-chak-chak, the massive black helicopter blades violently beat the air. The helicopter was only a few feet from the deck when the rough seas made the Naval ship list to the left hard.

The helo quickly ascended and hovered to regain its stability. Once the deck leveled out, it lowered itself again to land.

Right when he was about to land, I could see the aircraft's tail rotor about to touch the back of the ship. If it did, it would spin out of control and crash.

"Pull up, pull up," I commanded over the microphone to the pilot.

Being a Helicopter Control Officer comes with a lot of risk. My life and especially the lives of my sailors on the launch pad are in constant danger.

But the reward on the back end is greater. The risk associated with launching and recovering helicopters allows us to deliver essential parts, food to the ship and complete medical transfers.

Risk is probably the most frequent question I receive from investors, and naturally so. If you are investing thousands of dollars, you want to make sure our money is as "safe" as possible.

There is no reward without a little risk. No investment is guaranteed 100%.

The higher the projected return, the greater the risk (and vice versa). All the risks of an apartment deal are outlined in the Private Placement Memorandum (PPM).

But — multifamily investing is one of the safest, time-proven asset classes to invest in.

To be transparent: for active multifamily syndicators, our biggest risk will be any challenges we have with the risk of execution from the property management company or unforeseen market or property conditions. We mitigate this by selecting the BEST manager in the first place. This includes conducting background checks, on-site visits, professional interviews, speaking with referrals, and an in-depth review of the property manager's systems and processes. I like to take it a step further and ask them questions about hypothetical situations that could arise on the property and how they would respond.

My team and I also evaluate each deal conservatively and perform stress tests on the deal, such as how the property would perform under low occupancy rates, interest rates changes, low rent, expensive capital expenditures, a drop in Net Operating Income, or changes in exit cap rates. What we are looking for is how the multifamily property would perform under adverse conditions and modeling what it would take for the deal to go bad and actually fail.

There are hundreds of different ways to stress test a property under various situations. But, for the case of this book, I will focus on a few that are the most critical:

- **Low Tenant Occupancy:** The biggest impact to the income a property produces is how many units actually have tenants that pay rent. Street test to determine how low occupancy rates could go before the property cannot produce enough income to cover expenses and the debt service. This is also called the Breakeven Occupancy. It's the occupancy needed to maintain the minimum operations and keep the property running. We underwrite to assume a stable multifamily property will have a vacancy rate of around 5% to 6%, but how will the NOI be affected if the vacancy rate rose to 9% or 12%? What vacancy rate would drop the value of the apartment complex below the purchase price?

It's important that my team and I protect our investors' capital by looking at these potential impacts.

- **Low Rent From Projections:** When we underwrite a deal, we make projection assumptions on how much we can raise rents by, thus achieving a higher estimated Net Operating Income (NOI). But what happens if we expected to increase rents by $250 a unit but instead only achieved $100 or lower?
- **Exit Cap Rate:** Remember — the cap rate is the return we would expect to receive from an apartment complex if we paid all cash for it. Stress test that cap rates will be higher when you exit/sell the multifamily deal. It's conservative to assume that cap rates will rise between 0.2% to 0.25% per year. If we purchased at a 4% cap rate with a 3-year project hold, we should assume a 4.75% cap rate at exit. It's good practice to see how the value of the property and NOI is affected over a range of various cap rates. What we ultimately want to see is how high can the cap rate reach before selling would not be an option because the return to investors would suffer.
- If you are looking at a syndication deal and the operator projects the exit cap rate at sell to be lower than the cap rate at acquisition, that's a red flag. The operator is not being conservative in their underwriting.
- **Higher than normal Capital Expenditures (CAPEX):** Things always happen. Something will always go wrong. How would return projections be affected if CAPEX costs were higher than expected or delayed? What if we experienced other unforeseen maintenance issues such as plumbing, roof, mold, foundation, or electrical issues? We stress test to see how long the deal could hold up to unforeseen issues based on the estimated reserve budget.
- **Interest Rate Fluctuations:** What happens to return projections if interest rates rapidly rise before we can close on the property? Or, what if we are using bridge debt, and after completing value-add repairs, have to refinance and rates have drastically increased or we cannot qualify for a conventional lender

during a downturn in the economy? How would this affect the deal?

- **Net Operating Income Decrease:** How low could the NOI drop before returns to investors begin to be affected? What is the minimum NOI that must be achieved to pay LP(s) their pref?
- **Slow Market Growth:** No one can predict the future, and the real estate market is forever evolving and changing. We assume in our underwriting that rents will increase annually at around 3% to 4% and expenses at 1% to 2%. We stress test how the property's NOI will change with faster or slower growth rates. What happens if income declines to 2% and the expenses climb to 3%? As always, we are looking for the breaking point in the returns of the property and its ability to adequately supply returns to investors.

If any sponsor promotes that their returns are guaranteed, then that's a red flag: either they are a new, inexperienced operator or they are flat-out lying. Another thing to look out for are deals that are overly complicated. The return structure of the syndication should be simple for you as an investor to understand. If not, it's another sign that the Sponsors are new and or inexperienced or that the financial metrics of the deal itself are weak (so they are using creative strategies just to make it work).

To be straightforward: the risk passive investors face in syndications is limited. At worst, you would lose your original investment.

But that's still better than losing your house or a whole single-family investment property due to a market downturn.

For a more detailed list of red flags that investors should look out for when investing passively in syndications, scan the QR code or visit multifamilybytheslice.com.

Chapter 25

CAPITAL CALL

I discussed earlier that the initial investment from Limited Partners in a multifamily syndication is used to cover the down payment or any required renovations. There are, however, rare occasions where General Partners may ask the Limited Partners to contribute more capital into the deal to cover unexpected expenses or operations (we call this a capital call).

Great GP(s) would try to keep the deal alive with their own capital before asking for money from LP(s).

Although it is generally a negative perception when LP(s) are asked to participate in a capital call, below are several variable reasons why one may occur:

- The level of required renovations is greater than anticipated.
- Unexpected capital expenditures.
- The return metrics of the property are a lot lower than expected and are not efficient enough to cover the debt service and or operational expenses.

This could result from poor property management, inadequate marketing, crime, or other challenges. A capital call might be necessary to secure the appropriate funds to quickly complete exterior upgrades to fill units quickly or to boost marketing the apartment complex itself.

- A robust change in market conditions.
- A rapid increase in labor, material, and construction costs (shortages, price hikes, or a pandemic)
- The property business plan.
- Multifamily development and heavy value-add syndications are at the most risk of needing more capital to sustain the operations of a project.

It makes sense why LP(s) would have a distaste for being asked to participate in a capital call. This dilutes the reputation of the GP(s) and could be a sign that the Operators did not adequately perform due diligence or underwrite conservatively.

The Private Placement Memorandum (PPM) outlines what Limited Partners should expect if a capital call were to occur. This includes how they will be notified, when funds are due, and what happens if an investor refuses to or can't contribute.

Chapter 26

THE DIFFERENT WAYS TO FUND MULTIFAMILY DEALS

Lenders are your biggest investors as a Sponsor. Financing a large multifamily property is a lot different from the requirements used when purchasing a single-family home. When obtaining a residential mortgage, your ability to be approved is based on your own personal financial background and strength. Loan terms are typically the same, with a fixed 15 or 30-year amortization (the act of paying off debt with regular mortgage payments). Most people understand the residential side of debt. But commercial financing for multifamily can be more creative and complex. Instead of lending in a person's name like we typically see with residential, the name on the loan for a multifamily will typically be in the name of the property itself via a Limited Liability Company(LLC) — such as 456 Walnut Avenue. In regard to loan structure, commercial loans typically have a shorter lifespan, like 7, 10, or 15 years, with a 30-year amortization.

Unlike residential financing, where the value of a property is based on the comparable homes around it, commercial financing determines the value of a property based on the income it produces (Net Operating Income). Lenders will ask for all of the property's financials, to include leases, income statements, operating budgets, and pro formas. Underwriters are looking to see if the rental revenue will cover the debt service.

In real estate, debt is often broken down into two categories: non-recourse and recourse.

Non-recourse: A loan that uses the investment property itself as collateral if the borrower defaults. The GP(s) are not personally liable for the loan. Interest rates for these loans are higher because they expose lenders to more risk and have tighter approval requirements. This is the debt we prefer to have as Sponsors. The only time the loan would turn to recourse is if there was evidence of fraud or unethical behavior from the borrower. This is called bad boy carve-outs. It includes actions such as intentional negligence or criminal acts on the property that would cause it to be damaged or foreclosure, mortgage transfers without the consent of the lender, misappropriation of rents, or the misappropriation of insurance.

For example, if you purchased a 14-unit apartment complex in Phoenix, Arizona for $4 million, the debt would be secured by the property itself. If you failed to make loan payments, the lender could foreclose on the apartment as collateral to pay the remaining debt service. They could not go after any of your personal assets in court.

Recourse loan: I like to think of this as the recapture loan. If the borrower defaults, the bank may now go after the loan guarantor's savings and personal assets (think credit cards or auto loans).

For example, if you purchased a 20-unit apartment complex in Ohio, and if for some reason you could no longer afford to make the debt service payments, the lender would foreclose and sell the property to pay off whatever the outstanding loan balance is. If the property cannot be sold for a large enough amount to pay off the remaining debt service, then the lender has the right to go after the individual borrower's personal assets to cover the difference. Recourse loans are easier to finance and typically have a lower interest rate because lenders can go after personal assets besides having the property as collateral.

Whether the loan is non-recourse or recourse, limited partners are completely protected and bear no risk. At most, if a deal goes south, LP(s) could lose their initial investment.

Now that we have discussed the two basic types of debt, let's look into the four main financing strategies available to multifamily investors: agency debt, HUD, commercial mortgage-backed securities, and bridge debt. The type of debt you select for a property depends on the business plan.

Agency Debt: Just like the name implies, this loan is backed by government-guaranteed mortgage agencies Fannie Mae (Federal National Mortgage Association) and Freddie Mac (Federal Home Loan Mortgage Corporation) and is highly regulated. They usually have a lower LTV (loan to value) at 70-80% of the property purchase price with fixed-rate debt and are non-recourse. This is the opposite of a floating rate, where the interest changes over time. To be clear, LTV is the percentage amount that the lender agrees to let the buyer borrow against for whatever value the property appraised for. For example, a 75% LTV means that the General Partnership is putting down 25% in cash, and the remaining 75% would be borrowed from the lender based on the purchase price of the property. The benefit of this underwriting criteria is that it is conservative and keeps Sponsors from being over-leveraged.

To qualify for an Agency loan product, the net worth between GP(s) has to be equal to or greater than the loan balance and they need to have experience operating a property similar in size. This is the reason most syndications require a loan guarantor or Key Principal (KP) when properties are worth several millions of dollars. Another advantage of Agency debt is that the loans are assumable, allowing the buyer to basically take over the existing debt payments on the property.

Loan assumptions have not been a popular course of action or topic of discussion within the multifamily space for a while. Although purchasing an apartment with a loan assumption can be more complex, it also has a lot of great benefits. For one, it decreases the competition (because they aren't popular among investors) and increases your chances of finding a diamond deal. Two, depending on the numbers, it could actually be cheaper and allow an investor to acquire a multifamily property at a huge discount instead of attempting to purchase an apartment with a new loan.

Some of this complexity involves the lender itself; they are looking to see if the new borrower has the experience and balance sheet to acquire and operate the property. But most importantly, lenders want to have the warm and fuzzy feeling that the new borrower can safely assume the loan and make the appropriate payments without risk. This includes having a large amount of cash on hand to replenish taxes, insurance, and rental income/capex repair reserves.

Loan assumptions can be a huge advantage to buyers if the interest rate on the assumable loan is lower than what is currently available in the market. The opposite is also true. If interest rates across the market are low (which was the case recently during the COVID-19 pandemic), and thus less than what the assumable loan interest rate is, then it would not be wise to assume a loan. Assuming a loan with interest rates higher than the market also exposes the buyer to higher prepayment penalties.

Borrowers need to take the time to look into the interest-only payments (I/O) on the assumable loan when undergoing their research. There might be a chance that the I/O period of payments have ended or is about to end. If so, that means the debt payments will now be significantly larger and eat into the cash flow the property produces. This could turn a good deal into bad, especially if the complex still requires value-add renovations.

One last factor to consider is the loan expiration date. Buyers need to know how their business plan exit timeline aligns with when the loan is due.

The downside to Agency loans is banks will only lend to stabilized properties, which limits investors to mostly Class A and strong Class B properties. There is no option to fund renovations for agency debt like a bridge loan. The closest thing to achieving long term debt and being able to fund renovations would be using a loan product from smaller local banks/credit unions.

For securitized loans like Fannie Mae and Freddie Mac, there exist prepayment penalties known as yield maintenance. The actual prepayments consist of the loan's unpaid principal balance and an interest rate penalty on the total remaining interest the lender would have received over the full term of the loan. It basically repays the lender for all the income they would have received if the borrower(s) did not pay off their debt early. Most investors are fine with this increased risk of yield maintenance because they receive favorable terms and typically lower interest rates.

There is the option that if the owner wants to sell the property, they can do so and pass the existing debt service and yield maintenance prepayment penalty on to the new borrow through an assumable loan.

Another option available to sellers is to pay off the prepayment penalties early without transferring it to the buyer (known as defeasance). This is a strategy where the loan proceeds that the lender was guaranteed are replaced with treasury bonds that offer the same rate of return. It's critical that sellers hire professional defeasance consultants that can guarantee the treasury bonds they secure produce enough income to pay off the loan's interest and principal balance.

For those of you curious about how to calculate yield maintenance for a property, the formula is:

$$\begin{aligned} &\textit{Yield Maintenance} \\ &\quad = \textit{Remaining Mortgage Debt Balance} * (\textit{Interest Rate} \\ &\quad - \textit{Current Treasury Rate}) \end{aligned}$$

Commercial Mortgage-Backed Security (CMBS): Also commonly known as conduit loans, CMBS are non-recourse with a fixed rate (similar to Agency) but with more creative and less stringent underwriting approval criteria. Also, like Agency, interest rates are low and LTV leverage can extend up to 75%. As the name implies, loans are secured by the property itself, which is why lenders are less rigid with their underwriting and approval criteria. CMBS loans are created by banks. They take multiple commercial real estate loans (multifamily, retail, hotel, office, etc.) and group them together into a larger bucket. This is specifically done by a conduit (the intermediary that purchases the loans and sells the loans to investors). Last, this large bundle of loans is then sold to investors in a secondary market as bonds. The conduit is the intermediary individual that actually purchases, reviews, groups, securitizes into bonds, and sells the loans to the investors. Although this is happening in the background where loans are being resold on the secondary market, it doesn't affect the lending terms for the borrower.

Why does this matter?

Let's tie it all together with a brief example. Say a group of Operators come together to purchase a 40-unit apartment building. They go through the underwriting and qualification process and obtain a loan from a bank that allows them to purchase the apartment complex. The bank takes the Operator's new mortgage and groups it with other commercial mortgages they approved and turns them into bonds that are sold to investors (who receive regular fixed yield dividend payments for owning them). The bank earns money from selling the bonds to investors, and they use this new money to now lend to other future Operators. This process is known as loan securitization and is what makes qualifying for CMBS loans easier than Agency.

CMBS loans are best for Operators struggling to achieve financing through Frannie Mae and or Freddie Mac, but with properties that still have a decent stabilization and cash flow. Due to the structure of these loans — to use bond cash flow to pay off investors — it's not possible to prepay these loans, thus making a refinance or adding subordinate debt nearly impossible.

Department of Housing and Urban Development (HUD): There's a good chance that many of you have heard of the Federal Housing Administration (FHA), which allows people to purchase residential homes with a 3.5% down payment. Both programs have many similarities (high mortgage insurance premiums), except HUD is used for commercial assets like multifamily and moderate to low-income housing. HUD loans typically have a high LTV leverage 80-90%, competitive interest rates, prepayment penalties, can be assumable, are non-recourse with strict reserve and underwriting requirements, and have a 40-year amortization.

These loans are best for development syndication opportunities and distressed multifamily properties.

Bridge Debt: A short-term loan, usually between 1 to 2 years, that "bridges" you to eventually get more stable, secured, long-term debt.

The advantage of bridge loans is the application, approval, and funding are faster than that of Agency. This allows Sponsors to close a deal quickly if they need to, especially if investing in a highly competitive market. Another advantage of bridge loans is it is commonly used by Operators implementing a value-add business plan. Often, a good amount of the multifamily properties will have an occupancy rate below 85%. Remember: Fannie Mae and Freddie Mac will not lend on multifamily properties unless they at least have an 85% stabilized occupancy (or offer a low LTV at 60-65% due to the property's poor performance). Bridge loans allow operators to finance up to 80-90% of the rehab budget loan to cost (LTC). This is a great option for Sponsors because it allows them to close a deal and fund the majority of the costs required to complete renovations to raise occupancy and the income the property produces.

Although bridge loans usually have higher interest rates than Agency and HUD, many are interest-only (I/O), meaning that the payments are interest-only for a specific duration of the loan, and thus the debt service payment is lower. This is another huge advantage for General Partners because it allows us to make lower debt payments, which increases the cash flow the property produces and allows us to pay Limited Partners greater distributions. This is critical especially during a time when cash flow may be lower during renovations for a value-add business plan.

But there are some risks involved.

Despite all the advantages, the risk with bridge loans is after the usual 1 or 2-year loan term (can be longer on a case-by-case basis), the Sponsors are forced to refinance into more secure long-term debt or sell the property. No one has a crystal ball, but this could turn out risky if the market were to experience a downturn and CMBS or Agency financing is hard to get at the time when the Bridge loan term is over. If this happens, this could hurt and or change the projected returns of a syndication opportunity. The term (maturity of the loan) of the loan is crucial for a deal. You want the term of the loan to be longer than the hold period for the syndication opportunity to hedge against interest rate risk.

If Operators are using a bridge loan, they must have a solid plan for completing renovations and or getting occupancy at 85% or above to secure more permanent debt.

I know we went through a lot of comparisons between the financing options, so below is a table to summarize things.

	Leverage	Interest Rates	Downsides	Upsides
Agency	up to 80% LTV	competitive low rates	slow approval; yield maintenance; reserves required; loan does not fund renovations	non-recourse with bad boy carve-outs; assumable
HUD	up to 90% LTV	competitive rates	prepayment penalties; loan assumption/ refi is difficult; large reserves needed; slow approval	non-recourse; assumable; 40 year amortization; can have I/O payments
CMBS	up to 75% LTV	competitive low rates	prepayment penalties; no supplemental or refinancing available	non-recourse with bad boy carve-outs; assumable; easier approval process than Agency

Bridge	up to 90% LTC	High with I/O payments	short length; refinance required after 1-2 years	non-recourse; flexible terms, can fund capex/repairs, quick turnaround

Chapter 27

HOW TO FIND DEALS IN A COMPETITIVE MARKET

It's no surprise the real estate market has been more competitive than ever with interest rate fluctuations and an overabundance of material educating people on real estate, such as books, podcasts, mastermind groups, conferences, and YouTube videos. The multifamily space has become especially oversaturated, as many people recognize how safe and lucrative it is as an asset class. It has made finding good, cash-on-cash-yielding investment opportunities for Limited Partners more difficult.

The business concept Value-Add has especially been the most popular within the multifamily space. This is the sexy, popular term in the industry today, and many investors are overpaying on apartment buildings just to say they are completing a value-add deal.

This means that now more than ever, we have to be more creative in how we find and evaluate deals. So what criteria do we look for now?

1. Micro-units/ Micro-apartments

One way to stand out from the competition is to look at apartment complexes with micro (or mini) units. These units are about 350 square feet or smaller with a bathroom and or kitchen and have a tiny home feel. They are most common in urban areas. Large windows, high ceilings, or decks will make the units seem a lot larger than they actually are. They are a great option for investors to purchase units at a discount (price/per door). The units are studio size, with an open concept, which can be great for tenants because they are cheaper in rent and always in high demand. This allows Operators to easily control the occupancy. From a renovation standpoint, micro units are faster to complete and turn around. You could later on go back and combine one or two micro-units to make larger units but finding the deal itself will be easier if searching for micro-units alone.

I first saw this concept with my first syndication deal in San Diego, California. We bought a 12-unit apartment complex with all micro-units and 3 large common areas.

2. Mixed-use

Mixed-use is a building that has both residential and commercial tenants. Usually, there might be a coffee shop, store, doctor's office, etc., on the first floor, while the floors above are residential units. Ground or top-level retail mixed with apartment units in a complex steers away many investors because it's not as easy to analyze. Reading and understanding the commercial leases, insurance, taxes, and property management makes the underwriting a lot more difficult and time-consuming compared to easily plugging in 100% multifamily rents and income projections. This process could become even more complicated if the seller failed to adequately keep good financial records of the commercial space. Mixed-use is another great option to find great deals because having additional underwriting steps and a more complex analysis deters away a lot of Operators.

3. Unique Niche

As I mentioned before, demographic trends, competition, and tenant demand has produced a wave of new multifamily opportunities for investors. Below is a list of other unique niches within the multifamily space that can be exploited to find lucrative deals not overly competitive among other Operators. Some of these niches we invest in currently.

- Mini Syndications with Duplexes, Triplexes, and Fourplexes
- Co-Living/Co-Working
- Short Term Rentals in Multifamily
- Hotels converted into Multifamily
- Industrial spaces converted into Multifamily
- Manufactured Home Communities
- Condominium Units
- Additional Dwelling Units (ADUs) or Detached Additional Dwelling Units (DADUs)

4. Section 8

Overseen by the Department of Housing and Urban Development (HUD), Section 8 is a program created for low-income renters and families by the Housing and Community Development Act in 1974 to address the affordable housing crisis.

Many Operators are turned off by the label of Section 8 being for low income tenants and are scared there will be difficulties with residents paying rent or taking proper care of the units. This has been a controversial debate among real estate investors for decades. But, the truth is that Section 8 can be a profitable and reliable niche if done correctly. Section 8 tenants actually receive money from a voucher program that covers 70% of their rent and utilities. The tenants cover the other 30%.

Operators that wish to rent to Section 8 tenants would register with HUD to become approved as Section 8 landlords. The advantage of Section 8 is because the program is backed by HUD, investors are paid directly by the government via check or ACH every month. Sponsors will find comfort in knowing they would not have to deal with late tenant payments or even the nonpayment of rent (if a tenant were to stop paying due to financial hardship or negligence). Even if a tenant were to not pay their 30% portion of the rent, at least an investor still receives 70% of it each month instead of nothing. Another advantage is the free marketing and fast lease periods. Operators can list their apartment complex on the public housing authority (PHA) website and a verified waiting list of Section 8 tenants can apply for a unit. This helps maintain low vacancy rates in addition to the fact that most Section 8 tenants tend to stay in units for long periods of time. Section 8 tenants must complete regular inspections, which can help Operators fix damages and keep units in good condition. This is a plus compared to regular long-term leases where it could be a year before an investor can view a unit and find potential problems or fix necessary repairs. The last advantage of Section 8 is typically investors can achieve higher rents from Section 8 because you negotiate and determine the rent with the Section 8 office in advance. This is normally at market rent.

Section 8 can be another great option for investors to find good deals that most other Operators are not willing to touch.

5. **Unconventional, non-popular markets with large upside and potential**

Memphis, Austin, Dallas, San Antonio, and Phoenix have been some of the hottest real estate markets investors have turned to. What has resulted has been an over competition of Operators overpaying for a scarce selection of deals.

Instead, look at tertiary markets or other areas that are not popular among investors per say but that still offer strong economic metrics and returns. Examples include Los Angeles, Cabo San Lucas, Des Moines, Kansas City, Tulsa, Minnesota, Dayton, Mobile, etc.

See the trend here?

A large part of success as a multifamily investor goes into truly understanding your market and knowing ways to capitalize on trends or unique market dynamics to achieve cash flow.

6. **Student Apartments**

Similar to Section 8, multifamily student housing is another area in real estate that scares away many investors in fear that students will damage units or struggle to pay rent. People just seem to turn away from it immediately because they believe managing students is hard. But that's where a lot of great opportunities can be found, and you can easily have a third-party property management company manage the units. There are actually a lot of pros to investing in student rentals and they are a great option within the multifamily niche not overly saturated.

There is high demand for student housing among universities. Most can only offer housing to first-year students. To combat the shortage, developers and real estate investors are bringing more student apartments online for students to stay off-campus.

Despite what people think, student housing is actually recession-proof and has proven itself to be resilient in various downturns in the market. Even during the COVID-19 pandemic, when students were forced to go home and quarantine, multifamily student housing still performed well. Parents are often required to be on the lease for students as guarantors, so even when there is a recession or pandemic, they are still required to pay. This is another reason student housing is so lucrative. And even if the student is paying, because of how expensive school is and the fact they are attending classes for a serious purpose, they make sure to pay on time on the first of the month. It's the closest thing to guaranteed income. Another reason student apartments do well during a recession is that even in a bear market, people apply to school more because they believe by obtaining a new degree or certification, it will open up more job opportunities for them.

College students tend to have lower expectations and are easier to rent to than traditional renters. They care more about how close in proximity their unit is to campus and other amenities like coffee shops, restaurants, and stores. Marketing is easy for student housing due to the close proximity to campuses and built-in demand. Many students reach out instead, which allows for low vacancy rates. This doesn't even include the high demand from international students.

Enrollment and the need for education continue to increase. It's also easier to maintain rents at market levels because students move out every two, three, or four years. It doesn't matter how tight a city or state has rent control regulations. Even at market rents, on-campus room and board can still be more expensive, making living off-campus a very attractive option.

Compared to standard long-term leases, which are usually a year, student rentals have leases that are longer because of the degrees students are pursuing. It's not uncommon for a student to stay for a few years, especially if they plan to pursue higher levels of education like a master's or doctorate back-to-back.

As with any investment, there is risk. But student apartments can have some of the best returns in commercial real estate.

7. Senior Housing Apartments

Senior housing is apartments or facilities that provide care and living accommodations to older citizens. It is another low-risk, high-yield asset class that has performed well in several market cycles because it is a needs-based demand. The U.S population of senior citizens is set to double in the next 10 to 15 years. In 2022, over 60 million people were 65 or older. The increased mortality rate (due to healthcare and medical advances and people living more active lives), in addition to the aging population, explain the rapid rise.

Today, many senior apartments have waiting lists.

What's unique about senior apartments compared to other asset classes within real estate is the double component of hospitality and care services. Operators can even niche deeper within the senior housing asset classes by investing in age-restricted multifamily, independent living units, assisted living, memory care, and co-housing.

The tenants within senior housing offer stable, consistent, long-term rental income for several years.

Although senior apartments have excellent profit margins, what turns away most investors is the lack of experience and high operating costs. Senior housing requires an Operator to thoroughly understand safety and regulations, training and retaining staff, and how to manage a senior housing facility.

Chapter 28

WHAT IF I AM COMPARING TWO DIFFERENT SYNDICATION DEALS?

Don't just look at the numbers. I'm often approached by investors who will try to compare different deals based on the numbers. For example, there is not much of a difference between a 6% and 8% preferred return. I've seen this often: two active apartment investors analyzing the same deal will come up with different returns from their underwriting. What you'll find is the deal with the higher returns might be due to the Operator assuming from day one they would achieve 100% occupancy from the property, that they would be complete with any and all renovations within the first quarter, or that they used top-market pro forma rents. All three of these assumptions are beginner mistakes with underwriting.

Ultimately, you need to look deeper than just the plain numbers. You cannot pit and compare different multifamily syndications against one another based purely on return projections. Think about the story and the meaning behind the numbers and try to look for what will go wrong within any given deal. Again, I caution investors with shopping around deals for the highest return. This indicates that an Operator with the greatest return metrics is inflating their numbers and not being conservative in their underwriting — which is a risk for LP investors because it means they are not taking your capital investment seriously.

Other factors I would consider when comparing different syndication deals include General Partnership fees (fees should be reasonable and not over-inflated), profit split (what share of equity and profits do investors receive? 70/30? 80/20?), exit plan (look at the overall hold period and the plan for disposition), and taxes (whether a cost-segregation study was performed or not).

Last, some apartment syndications will give the Limited Partners voting rights for large decisions regarding the property, such as restructuring returns, changing property management, or the death/ transfer of existing investors.

Although the metrics discussed above are important, you should ultimately pick a deal based on the Sponsors.

Character and being ethical — not IRR, equity multiple, and large preferred returns — are what matter most.

I have met Limited Partners who have invested in some of my syndication deals that were burned in the past by other Operators. I'm always saddened to hear they had bad experiences with other Syndicators. It's worth looking into the criminal history and completing a Google search on each General Partner. Consider asking the GP(s) for referrals to speak with investors from their previous deals.

Chapter 29

WHAT EXACTLY DOES IT MEAN TO ADD VALUE TO AN APARTMENT?

Most of us are familiar with the concept of flipping a single-family home. Basically, a Value-Add business plan is essentially a long flip for an apartment complex over several years. We touched on this concept briefly earlier in the book. But now, we will explore this concept further. Examples of adding value to an apartment complex include upgrading kitchens to granite countertops, energy-efficient lights and water systems, laminate flooring, new carpet, modern cabinets, smart thermostats, updating the clubhouse or gym, renovating the pool area, adding a dog park, covered parking, repainting the exterior, and or rebranding the apartment complex.

The last way GP(s) add value is by decreasing expenses. These items include property management, maintenance & repairs, payroll, landscaping, and utilities (one flat fee all tenants pay or a bill-back system). Most Value-Add deals are B & C class properties.

Let's consider a 117 apartment complex as an example in Phoenix, AZ. Assuming a tenant occupancy of 95% and market cap rate of 4%, the property produced a total Net Operating Income (after all expenses excluding the debt service) of $1,200,000. This equates to a property value worth $30 million.

How did I get a value of $30 million? Well, remember our NOI equation from before?

Apartment Value = Net Operating Income (NOI) /Cap Rate

Thus, $1,200,000/0.04 = $30,000,000.

THE ENCLAVE APARTMENT COMPLEX	
Number of Units	117
Net Operating Income (NOI)	$1,200,000 (annually)
Market Cap Rate	4%
Property Value	$30 million

Now, using the same 117 complex, let's take this example further and say that as Operators, we identified a desire among residents to have valet trash service available. Let's assume we implemented this additional valet trash service for every unit at an additional $15 per unit. By just adding an additional $15 of income per unit, we added $526,500 in additional equity into the value of the property. The overall value of the 117-unit rose from $30,000,000 to $30,526,500.

Pretty Cool, Right?

	Valet Trash Service	**The ENCLAVE**
Additional Income per Unit	$15	
Increase in NOI	$1,775 (month) or $21,060 (annually)	$1,221,060

Increase in Property Value	$526,500	$30,526,500

Adding valet trash service was just one way to boost the income. What if we added other amenities to the property besides improving the unit interiors/exteriors? Let's assume that after making unit upgrades, we raised rents by an additional $200.

Here's how that would look.

	Unit Upgrades	**The ENCLAVE**
Additional Income Per Unit	$200	
Increase in NOI	$23,400 (month) or $280,800 (annually)	$1,501,860
Increase in Property Value	$7,020,000	$37,546,500

If we raised rents by $200 a unit, that would boost the NOI to $280,800 [(117 units*$200)*12 months in a year) and add a whopping $7 million in additional equity ($280,8000/0.04). As you can see, as Operators, we have direct control of the value of the property by making creative, strategic improvements.

Typically, you make renovations to the vacant units first because it's the easiest way to start with no tenants in place. Next, as other leases expire within the complex, you upgrade those. This cycle continues in a loop to complete the rest of the renovations. Usually, most residents are happy to pay the higher market rent with the upgraded units because they can see the huge change in added amenities and quality of the units themselves.

Chapter 30

PROPERTY AND LOCATION CLASSIFICATIONS

When evaluating the risk, quality, and potential of an investment property, Sponsors consider the grade classification. Although there is no exact, industry-standard rating criteria, most properties and neighborhoods are categorized and marketed based on an A, B, C, or D rating class (think of a report card). Real estate professionals will have different ambiguous definitions for each class, but in general they are:

- **A Class:** Newer, premium properties in a great location with good schools, businesses, low crime, coffee shops, and grocery stores.

Class A properties are best suited for investors seeking immediate cash flow (preservation). This is a safe, stable investment with lower appreciation because the asset is a newer build (10 to 15 years old) with high-end/modern appliances, finishes, and amenities. Investors can expect to see a preferred return of around 6% to 8% for a Class A deal. The pref is lower because the risk is lower. Class A properties achieve high rental rates, have a higher caliber of tenants, are recession-resistant, hedge great against inflation, have limited downside, and have low expenses or no deferred maintenance. There is little room to implement a value-add strategy for Class A assets.

- □ **B Class:** Properties built within the last fifteen to thirty years with minor wear and tear. This is considered the middle ground for investment properties because, typically, the properties are in decent shape. Expenses are a little bit higher for repairs due to the slightly older age. The amenities and rental rates are a step below Class A, and the tenant mix usually reflects those with good, stable jobs such as government employees, hospital workers, military, etc. Class B properties typically do well during an economic downturn (limited downside).

Good location with great shopping centers and retail, but not as fancy as Class A. Could be a great opportunity for the Valued-Add strategy depending on the condition and or age.

- □ **C Class:** Older properties built more than thirty years or newer buildings that are rundown. C Class neighborhoods are considered working-class/blue-collar with older amenities. You can still find properties in good condition and in good neighborhoods needing minor repairs/remodeling for Class C. This is the bread and butter for real estate investors because they usually have the greatest upside for the Value-Add business plan. Many of the interior and exterior components can be upgraded to then increase and achieve rents right below Class B properties.

Class C properties have an average, moderate performance during low economic cycles.

- □ **D Class:** Distressed properties. High crime, non-desirable living area with little to no grocery stores or green space. This is the riskiest property and location to invest in. These properties are old with considerable amounts of deferred maintenance/repairs.

I would be cautious of Class D property deals unless the General Partnership team has experience with this asset class in particular.

Chapter 31

HOW DO WE KNOW WHEN TO SELL?

General Partners sell early if they feel the deal is near a peak or if returns are far greater than what was originally projected to the Limited Partners.

There may be cases where completing a refinance to return most of (or all of) Limited Partners original investment may be a better option. This scenario usually occurs when the renovations from a Value-Add business plan have been completed and the Net Operating Income (NOI) has increased substantially. A refinance may also be a good play for Sponsors to achieve more favorable debt service terms, which also increases the cash flow output of the deal.

Note: Even when a refinance is made and LP(s) initial capital is returned, they still receive a preferred return and will participate in the equity split upside when the deal is later sold.

One question I have been asked by many investors is what about a long term hold play where the multifamily property is held for several years?

This could be achieved if the GP team made several refinances over the life of the project to continue to return capital back to investors besides the regular, consistent, pref they would receive. However, the biggest downside to this long-term hold approach is that selling would allow LP(s) to take advantage of earning the highest return on capital they could achieve. When you sell, GP(s) normally achieve a higher sale price than the evaluation the bank would give for the property for a refinance. Thus, yielding lower refinance proceeds. Selling the property would allow the LP(s) to roll their proceeds into another investment opportunity.

It's clear there are multiple options to choose from on how to exit or hold a multifamily syndication deal. As General Partners, my team and I are constantly evaluating when the best time to sell is and what option would yield the greatest return for our Limited Partners.

Chapter 32

FREQUENTLY ASKED QUESTIONS

At the end of the webinar, when a syndication deal is presented, or throughout the life of a project, a few questions remain common and stand out to me. Some I have addressed already within the book, but I'd still like to go over again a few of the most common questions I receive from investors.

Are you still paid as a GP if the deal is performing poorly?

No, General Partners are not paid if a deal is performing badly. Limited Partners must be paid their preferred return first before Sponsors are paid anything.

How can I discover future investment opportunities?

To be notified about future investment opportunities, you must be a part of our mailing list. To join the That's My Property mailing list, visit drmultifamily.com

Once subscribed, as new investment opportunities become available, they will be sent out via email.

What is your stance on losing an investor's money? What would you do? What happens if there is a recession/pandemic? Have you ever had to do a capital call?

We have never had to conduct a capital call.

If we did lose investors' money, the General Partnership would make every effort to utilize their own money to keep the deal afloat and or pay Limited Partners their initial investment back.

We take investors' capital very seriously. To help avoid this, we employ the following tactics to avoid losing investors' money during a financial crisis or pandemic:

- Increase communication to bi-weekly
- Stop or reduce the preferred return and pay investors back their pref via a catch up later within the deal
- Stop renovations being completed to build cash reserves
- Stop or delay any capital expenditures that are unnecessary to the sustained operation of the property
- Increase tenant occupancy by offering promotions and concessions.
- Offer promotions and concessions to current tenants whose leases are about to expire to retain high tenant residency.
- Contact lenders about possible refinance or supplemental loans to tap into the equity in the property for further cash reserves
- Look into possible government assistance programs

When do I get my original investment back?

Typically, during a refinance or when the deal is sold. We like to sell around years 3 or 5, depending on market dynamics. Remember, we might hold even longer for up to 7 or 10 years if there is a downturn in the economy.

What if I have an emergency or hardship and need my money back?

This will be handled case-by-case with the General Partners. However, Limited Partners should not invest their last bit of money in a syndication at the risk they have no more funds in case of an emergency. Investors should view their investment within a syndication as illiquid.

How do you renovate and make upgrades while people are living at the property?

We start with the vacant units first. Even a 100-unit apartment complex with an occupancy above 95% will have vacant units. Once the vacant units are renovated, we move new tenants in those units and move to renovating the next 10-15 leases that just ended — and so on. We continue repeating this process until we achieve the desired pro forma income as projected in our business plan.

What happens to my investment if the economy is in a downturn?

Multifamily properties hold up well during a downturn. However, Sponsors will commit to continue paying our investors their preferred return and wait to sell the asset when the timing is right.

In what ways is your underwriting of a deal conservative?

As General Partners, our goal is to always under-promise and over-deliver for our investors. I've seen many deals where Sponsors advertise their rental income projections to be at market levels or aggressively above. This should be avoided; you always want your rents to be slightly under the market value even after making renovations. This is not only conservative but allows the property to be extremely competitive by offering high-quality units to tenants at rental rates slightly below market level.

We estimate modest rental growth and perform a sensitivity analysis. This allows us to show our investors multiple worst-case scenarios such as low occupancy, low rents, cap rate changes, high expenses, and how the property would perform as a result. To give you an idea, our conservative underwriting usually allows occupancy to go to 70 to 75% in order to break even and still be safe. Multifamily properties have averaged above 85% occupancy levels for the past 15 years. Vacancy has never dropped below 80%. Investors should find great comfort in this.

What would be a reason someone wouldn't want to invest in a particular syndication deal?

There could be a number of reasons Limited Partners may not want to invest in a particular deal. However, a few reasons could involve: investors may be hesitant to invest in a deal with Operators that are inexperienced, have projected returns that seem inflated and or unrealistic, lack of knowledge or fear, or they may not like the particular market where the deal is located.

What if investor distributions are delayed or missed?

Distributions would be caught up and paid to investors at a later time during the lifecycle of the syndication deal or at sale.

Who can I contact if I have questions?

You can contact any of the General Partners if you have questions. Contact information will be at the bottom of all emails and within the Private Placement Memorandum.

How are investors kept up to date on the process or financials of the property?

Limited Partners will receive monthly or quarterly email updates on the property's performance. This includes pictures, renovations (if applicable), rent collections, repairs, etc. Quarterly property management financials will also be provided.

Chapter 33

THE ETHICS OF MULTIFAMILY & BUILDING COMMUNITIES

The government shut down during the spring of my freshman year at the Naval Academy. With no funding, many trips the Academy normally offered to midshipmen were canceled.

One thing was for certain: my parents begged my brothers and me not to come home.

Murders and shootings, much of it gang-related, had escalated on the South Side. I recall the conversation on the phone with my stepfather clearly. "Andre, over 40 people were shot over the weekend. I can't wait to leave this place." In my parents' eyes, with so much to lose, they feared we would come home and be shot. I never understood this logic entirely. I got their concern, but what about their safety? My mind constantly thought about their well-being when I first left home. It was a hard pill to swallow, but I was miles away and there was nothing I could do to protect them. At some point, I had to just let go — I couldn't continue to carry the burden of worrying about my parents. All I could do was pray and trust that God would watch over them. Even in a different state, with so much negative media attention surrounding Chicago, it was hard not to be constantly reminded that my time at the Naval Academy was a blessing. In the end, Triad Christian Fellowship (TCF), a bible study I attended weekly at the Naval Academy, had a spring break trip scheduled. The group's leader, Connor, received word of our situation. TCF paid for my brothers and my expenses to attend. It was our first time out of the country.

When I envisioned my mission trip to Jamaica, I pictured myself building homes and feeding people, not walking into prison cells.

We went to prison.

Mr. Orneal, our bible study leader, took my friends and me to Tower Street Adult Correctional Center in Kingston, a brown brick and concrete facade reminiscent of a castle. The fortress had large sentry towers and 20 feet walls that extended toward the street. Multiple rolls of barbed razor wire stretched along the walls. Tower St. was the largest correctional center in Jamaica, home to adult males and juveniles. I, a former gang member in Chicago, and my friend Stewart, from the streets of Atlanta, were chosen to speak to the men. The rest of our group spoke to the juveniles.

What happened next challenged my perspective on life.

Mr. Orneal escorted our group through a security checkpoint and multiple thick metal gates. My eyes roamed around, taking in the new scenery. I turned around.

The motto of the prison was painted in big bright red letters: *NONE SHALL ESCAPE.*

My feet slapped against the hard, dirty concrete floor as I approached the chamber. When we walked in the dark cell, Stewart and I stood before a group of men. The cells were the size of a small one-car garage with a toilet in the ground. I remember their faces. The look in their eyes. It was evident that no one could mentally prepare for the nightmare of harsh prison conditions. I could feel their judgment. To break the ice, Stewart and I opened up the conversation by introducing ourselves and our backgrounds. "Wassup fellas, many of you are probably wondering what right I have to stand before you and speak. I don't. I can't pretend to understand what your life is like here in prison. What I can speak from is the impact gangs, poverty, and violence had on me growing up in Chicago." Almost immediately, the cloud of judgment faded. The tense upward placement of their shoulders relaxed; the bent aggression of their frowned eyebrows eased. I watched the dramatic change in body language and curiosity kindle as the group of men struggled to logically understand how two men could transition from the streets to the Naval Academy.

It was special. Looking into their eyes, I saw myself. What stood before us were not killers, thieves, or menaces to society, but promising men struggling to figure life out because they lacked adequate resources and, most importantly, love. Without hesitation, the men asked various questions, such as how I got out of the gang, details of different incidents I had been through in Chicago, and life as a midshipman at the Naval Academy.

This was the first time I openly spoke about my past, let alone to people in a different country.

The new experience itself felt weird. Realizing how much these young men looked up to me, I knew one of my callings: using my story to help inspire others.

Today that has transformed into giving back and transforming people's lives through real estate.

One thing I am passionate about is the ethics and outreach that come with being a multifamily investor. Just like a Naval Officer, you have a duty and unique opportunity to use your position to impact the lives of others.

One question I have had investors ask me, or concerns that I'll hear others talk about, is raising the rents on tenants. The Value-Add business model is about improving the interiors and exteriors of the property and raising rental rates. Some tenants may not be able to afford the higher prices and thus will have to leave.

And it's at that moment where true character comes into play.

The ethical thing to do as an Operator is to speak to every tenant that cannot pay the higher rent and help assist them. This could be paying for their moving expenses or working with them until they find another place to stay.

One of the true benefits of being a multifamily investor is your impact on the community: directly and indirectly.

Directly, you raise the value of the neighborhood by improving a large apartment complex that adds to the beautification of the community. You can host real estate outreach events at the property to inspire and educate youth, book club readings for kids and young adults, using the common areas to host seminars on educational topics or lectures on important topics such as mental health or wellness. Adding a nice gym to the complex and hosting classes there once a month could help boost and promote mental health and physical fitness. You could have a tutoring or education center made on the complex to help youth with education and or their homework. You could host food drives or tenant community volunteer events. You could host networking events at the complex for young adults and or business professionals, small college fairs, or jobs fairs. There could even be a daycare center added.

The possibilities are endless.

Indirectly, you can also help support charities by directing a portion of the profits from the syndication deal to mental health, education, veterans, and youth charities.

As you can see, multifamily real estate investors have a powerful ability to inspire others and uplift communities in many creative ways. We are able to add value and raise the income of a property, and still make a solid profitable business move, while helping and serving others.

I do not take this opportunity lightly.

Chapter 34

IT'S TIME TO GO TO THE NEXT LEVEL

> *"The best time to plant a tree was 20 years ago.*
> *The second best time is today."*
> *– Ancient Chinese Proverb*

Congratulations! By reaching this point, you have learned a great deal about multifamily real estate. Having the knowledge and how to apply it is one thing, but what separates the good from the great and those that actually achieve results — is action.

In this book, I've laid out the steps I took to get into multifamily real estate. I showed you that investing in real estate is a beautiful thing and a powerful tool. I showed you that most of you actually want to, and are best suited to, be passive investors. I also gave you a crash course on multifamily syndications and how to invest in them.

Nothing I taught you within this book is beyond you. If you read through the book and made it this far, I know you can move forward and make your first investment. You have demonstrated that you have what it takes.

Remember, fear is just a GPS for where our hearts most want to go. If investing in multifamily syndications intimidates you, then that really just means you are on the verge of something great and monumental.

If multifamily syndications can work for a former gang member from the South Side of Chicago, then it can work for you too. Don't just hear what I am saying. I am giving you an invitation. Our greatest struggles are within ourselves. When I go into neighborhoods and schools to speak to the youth, it has always bothered me that I can pour so much into them, and only a handful will actually implement what I have spoken about. At the end of each motivational speech, many come up to me inspired — yet few actually act on my words. I'm wired to care, and I am passionate about helping others and adding value to people's lives.

Just like the kids and young professionals I speak to, I worry that some of you will read this and be inspired but ultimately fail to move forward and act. The sad truth is that some of you will still fail to act and find an excuse after reading this.

Therefore, I CHALLENGE you. Do not waste the feelings of inspiration and motivation you feel right now. Leverage them and act TODAY. Go to my website, book a call with me, and learn what you need to do to invest in your first apartment syndication with me.

I can't wait to have you join the That's My Property family and invest alongside us in multifamily syndications. This will be a fantastic, profitable journey. There's a reason why so many people love Marvel comics and movies. We are all searching for a way to be a hero in some way. Everyone has some type of hero in their lives they look up to. If you take the lessons in this book to heart and commit to investing in multifamily syndications, then YOU can be that hero for your family, loved ones, and others. It's time to begin your hero's journey into the world of apartment investing and leave a greater influence on the world.

Say it with me: *That's My Property!*

Chapter 35

THE OPPORTUNITY TO ADD VALUE

"There are people less qualified than you, doing things you want to do, simply because they decided to take action."
– Anonymous

Ready to move forward and invest in multifamily real estate with me? Check out my website at drmultifamily.com. There you can join the *That's My Property* Tribe and enjoy the fruits of investing in apartment buildings. I receive so much joy from helping other people make money and live a more fulfilled life!

Check out and subscribe to my weekly podcast, *Multifamily by the Slice.* On this show—one slice of wisdom at a time—you'll gain unique perspectives from investors and professionals on all aspects of the apartment investing space. The podcast is available on all major streaming platforms: Spotify, Apple Podcasts, iHeartRadio, Audible, Google Podcasts, Stitcher, and Amazon Music.

If you are a beginner looking to learn more about real estate, a passive investor, or an active real estate investor within the Southern California area, I invite you to attend the #1 Real Estate Meetup Group in

San Diego County: Opportunity Knocks. The guest speakers that my team and I bring in have decades of experiences from various perspectives, and a passion for doing good. We'll be bringing you live deals, interviews with subject matter experts, and other salient content. This community is designed for you to not only network and learn from others within the commercial real estate industry, but to build lasting genuine relationships.

You can join and learn more about Opportunity Knocks by scanning the following QR code.

Follow me on Instagram, LinkedIn, Facebook, and Twitter(@ drmultifamily) if you are interested in learning more about my story, my passion for helping others, or for motivational posts to help inspire you to become a bigger and better version of yourself. There is also a ton of Value-add content I post for those of you interested in investing in multifamily real estate, such as videos, podcasts, quote cards, and engaging graphics.

Before you go, I have one last challenge for you. The two most powerful words in the dictionary are: I AM. Thus, repeat after me:

I AM capable of being a person of value.
I AM capable of achieving all my financial dreams.
I AM abundant.
I AM a giver.
I AM wealth.
I AM an overcomer.
I AM grateful.
I AM ready.
I AM an investor in apartment syndications.

KEY TERMINOLOGY

Investors, podcasts and meetup guests, and people I have met along the way often struggle with grasping the vocabulary that encompasses multifamily real estate. Half the battle in the learning and investing process is understanding the language we speak. Thus, this key terminology section was created as a foundational reference for readers. I hope it provides you great value.

I encourage you to refer to this list anytime you encounter a word you are not familiar with or can't remember what it means. A few tips to effectively learn vocabulary include flashcards, writing them out on a dry erase board, speaking to someone about them and using the words in context, memory techniques, repeating them out loud to yourself, etc.

A

Accredited Investor: An individual that can invest in real estate syndications with an annual income of $200,000 (or $300,000 for joint income with a spouse) or a net worth of at least $1 million (not including their primary residence).

Absorption Rate: The number of rental units leased over a period of time. Used by investors, lenders, brokers, and property managers to determine apartment market or property trends.

Adjustable Interest Rate Loan: A loan in which the interest rate and payments float or change multiple times during the term of the loan.

Appraisal: What a property's market value is based on its location, condition, and sales comparable within the area. How much a lender will lend on the purchase of a property.

Agency Debt: Long-term, typically low-interest-rate loans backed by government-sponsored enterprises Fannie Mae or Freddie Mac.

Acquisition Fee: Fee paid to General Partners in a syndication for all the work required to underwrite and close on a property.

Active Investing: Like another job, an investor who is consistently hands-on in finding and managing real estate investment opportunities.

Amortization: Paying off debt over a set period. A portion of each payment goes toward the loan principal and another toward the interest. The amount of money applied to the principal book value starts out small but grows larger over time each month.

Appreciation: The increase in value of a property over time or through forced improvements.

Assumption Fee: The fee a buyer pays when assuming the debt service of a property not completely paid off.

Asset Management Fee: A monthly or quarterly recurring fee paid to the General Partners in a syndication for managing the property (funded from the property income).

B

Bridge Loan: A short-term loan commonly used in Value-Add multifamily to fund repairs and renovations when occupancy levels may be low or Agency debt is not an option.

Basis Points (BPS): The unit of measure for interest rates and percentages. One basis point is 1/100th of 1%. For example, 50 basis points is 0.5% and 1 basis point is 0.01%.

Bad Debt: Unpaid rental income that property owners are unable to collect.

Breakeven Occupancy: The tenant occupancy rate needed to cover all the expenses of an apartment complex.

Bad-Boy Carve-Outs: Provisions written within non-recourse loan documents that protect the lender from the dishonest actions of a borrower. These bad boy actions include bankruptcy, falsifying documents, criminal acts done purposely on the property by the borrower, failure to pay taxes, failure to maintain insurance, or any other malicious acts completed referring to the borrower and the loan. The provisions state that if the borrower violates the terms of the loan, they will be held personally liable for the existing balance of the loan.

Bond: Security investments that produce fixed-income cash flow from loans. They are secured by the real estate property itself.

Broker: An individual that is a licensed real estate professional that represents buyers or sellers in commercial real estate transactions.

C

Capital: Cash or liquid assets.

Carried Interest: See definition on Promote.

Cash Flow: In real estate, the total profit a property produces each month after paying all operating expenses and debt service.

Cost Approach: One of three methods used to determine the value of a rental property. This method calculates what the value of a property would be based on its rebuild cost if it was destroyed (cost of land + construction costs).

Concessions: Discounts or promotions (such as rent, parking, and or storage) given to new or existing tenants to entice them to stay or sign a lease.

Closing Costs: Costs paid by the buyer of a property (usually 2-5% of the loan amount) to cover origination and underwriting feeds, commissions, taxes, legal, and insurance premiums.

Crowdfunding: Funding a project or real estate venture by raising money from a large group of people or donors (this has become easier and increased with the internet).

Customer Relationship Management (CRM): Using a platform or automation tool to provide marketing, networking, customer service, support, and or sales to Limited Partners or General Partners.

Capitalization Rate (Cap rate): The rate of return a property would be expected to produce if you paid all cash for it.

Capital Expenditures (CapEx): Money used to buy, repair, or maintain big-ticket assets on a property that extends its useful life (such as a roof, foundation, plumbing systems, electrical systems).

Cash on Cash Return (CoC): The estimated annual return on cash flow from a property by dividing the cash flow earned by the initial cash investment.

Cost Segregation: A tax strategy used to reclassify and break exterior and interior building components into short life spans to defer taxes and reduce the tax liability of an apartment complex. In a syndication, the benefits can be passed down to the Limited Partners.

Capital Stack: A layered ladder that portrays the organization and payout priority of the different funding sources used to purchase a property. It outlines who receives the debt and equity in a financed property and in what order.

D

Debt Service: The loan payment required to pay the principal and interest for a set period of time to a lender.

Disposition: Another way of saying that a property is being sold.

Debt Service Coverage Ratio (DSCR): A ratio lenders use to determine how much income a property must produce to cover the debt service and qualify for financing. Lenders require a minimum DSCR of 1.25 to issue a loan.

Depreciation: The decrease in value of a property over time and an income tax deduction that allows investors to deduct the cost of buying or improving a property.

Defeasance: A commercial loan prepayment penalty where an investor exchanges a positive cash-producing asset (such as a Treasury security) with the property as loan collateral.

Due Diligence: A term used to describe when an investor or group of partners performs investigative audits on a property's underwriting, financial reports, inspections, surveys, management, repairs, title, legal, taxes, etc.

Distributions: Money paid to investors monthly or quarterly in and or at exit from a real estate syndication deal.

Drop & Swap: Dropping out of one investment opportunity to exchange or swap into a new real estate investment deal.

Driving for Dollars: The act of driving around to look at properties to find off-market deals.

E

Equity Multiple: How much an investor would gain on their initial investment in a real estate syndication. Calculated by dividing the total investor cash distributions by the initial equity invested in a deal. A multiple of 2x means an investor doubled their money. A multiple of 1x means they broke even.

Equity Investment: The initial capital an investor contributes to a syndication.

1031 Exchange: Section 1031 of the U.S Internal Revenue Code. A tax-deferral strategy that allows investors to defer capital gains tax from selling a property by reinvesting the profits from sale (within 180 days) into one or a group of like-kind properties of equal or greater value.

Earnest Money Deposit: Money placed into escrow (usually 1-2% of the purchase price) by a buyer to indicate to the seller their commitment to execute on purchasing the apartment complex.

Education Savings Account (EDA): An account that allows parents to save (tax-deferred) for child elementary, secondary, and higher-level education tuition, fees, and other expenses through various investment options such as real estate, stocks, bonds, mutual funds, and money market funds.

Effective Gross Income (EGI): The actual true income a property generates after subtracting unit vacancies, loss to lease, and credit losses, from the total income (rental income + other income sources such as vending, laundry, parking, etc.).

Economic Occupancy Rate: The rate of actual income received from tenants based on occupancy.

Exit Strategy: How the General Partnership plans to return capital to investors. This is usually through selling the property or a refinance.

Expense Ratio: A conservative metric is to have an expense ratio of 50% when analyzing a multifamily property. Expense ratio is calculated by dividing total expenses by total income. This ratio is a quick metric that portrays how efficient a property operates.

F

Forced Appreciation: Increasing the value and income of an apartment complex by raising rental rates from exterior and interior upgrades and decreasing operational expenses.

G

General Partners (GP): The quarterbacks of an apartment syndication. They are overall in charge of finding a property, placing it under contract, communicating with investors, and operating the business plan successfully.

Gross Potential Rent (GPR): The hypothetical maximum amount of income a property would produce at 100% occupancy with market rate rents.

Gross Rent Multiplier (GRM): The number of years it would take for a property to pay for itself based on the income it produces.

H

Holding Period: The total time General Partners plan to operate the syndication deal.

Hard Commit: When an investor officially secures their spot in a real estate syndication deal by signing the Private Placement Memorandum (PPM) documents and wiring their investment funds into the syndication bank account.

Health Savings Account (HSA): A tax-advantaged medical account used to save up for medical expenses by investing in various asset classes and securities such as real estate, stocks, and bonds.

I

Interest-Only Payment (I/O): A commercial loan where monthly payments are interest-only for a set period. This is common among bridge loans and for General Partners that want to preserve more capital to use for renovations and repairs. It also allows General Partners to pay Limited Partners good returns at the start of a Value-Add deal while renovations are being made because the debt service is significantly less for the first few months or years.

Internet Rate: How much a lender charges a borrower for using their funds to finance a real estate deal.

Investor Portal: An online portal that General Partners use to raise capital from and deliver statements, tax documents, and other property information to Limited Partners in a syndication offering.

Investor Relations (IR): The consistent communication of the General Partnership with Limited Partners in a syndication deal, such as property updates, distributions, and or answering questions.

Internal Rate of Return (IRR): The overall time rate of return of an investor's money.

J

Joint Venture (JV): A simple partnership among two to four persons who have come together to purchase a real estate investment property together.

K

K-1: IRS Form 1064 U.S. Return of Partnership Income. An annual report that depicts each General Partners and Limited Partners' profits, losses, deductions, distributions, and ownership percentage in a real estate syndication. Losses from bonus depreciation are passed through from the apartment complex LLC entity to Limited Partners and are reported on the K-1 as well.

Kep Principal (KP): Also known as a Guarantor. A person who offers up their balance sheet of assets to get the General Partnership team to qualify for a loan. It is standard that their net worth must at least be equal to the loan balance of the syndication property. In exchange, they receive a guarantee fee at closing or receive a small equity stake in the deal.

L

Limited Partner (LP): A passive investor in a syndicate offering.

Letter of Intent (LOI): A non-binding agreement sent to a seller by a buyer stating their intent to purchase a property and their proposed purchase terms.

Leverage: Using debt borrowed from a lender to purchase a property and increase its income and or value.

London Interbank Offered Rate (LIBOR): The benchmark interest rate average that banks use to calculate loan interest rates. It is calculated from the estimates submitted by the major banks in London based on how much they would be charged to lend short-term loans to one another.

Loss to Lease (LTL): The difference in price between a rental unit's market rate and what it actually rents at per the signed lease agreement.

Loan to Cost Ratio (LTC): A ratio that compares the total costs of a construction/renovation for a property to the anticipated loan amount.

Loan to Value Ratio (LTV): A ratio that compares the debt service on a mortgage to the appraised value of a property. Lenders often use this metric to help evaluate the risk of lending funds to a borrower.

Lease Option: An agreement between the property owner and tenant that after a predetermined time period, the renter has the option to purchase the property at an agreed-upon price. The owner is not able to sell the property to anyone else within that period. If the renter does not execute the option to purchase they must forfeit it.

M

Market Rent: The market value of a unit based on what other rental units are leasing for within the area.

Mezzanine Debt: Non-traditional financing in between senior debt and equity. It's a hybrid way to finance deals because lenders have the option to convert the debt into equity ownership within a property as well. It's a creative form of financing that combines debt and equity for lenders. Usually used to maximize the leverage employed to acquire an investment property or to better qualify for a first position mortgage. Interest rates are typically higher, but with flexible repayment options.

Metropolitan Statistical Area (MSA): A geographical region that consists of a large city of 50,000 or more and several other high population density areas surrounding it. Examples would be New York, Dallas-Fort Worth, Tampa, Los Angeles, and Houston.

Model Unit: A vacant unit used as a sales tool to show potential tenants what an actual apartment unit looks like within the complex.

Multifamily: A fancy way of saying apartment. Multiple separate housing units for residents.

N

Net Operating Income (NOI): The golden standard in calculating the profit and value of a commercial real estate property. The total revenue from a property minus its operating expenses. Debt service is not included as an operating expense.

Non-Recourse Loan: A loan not personally guaranteed by the borrower. If the borrower defaulted, the lender could only pursue the real estate property as collateral.

O

Offering Memorandum: Also known as the Private Placement Memorandum. A document that outlines the terms, risks, and business plan for a real estate syndication deal.

Operating Expenses: The costs necessary to run and maintain the daily operations of an apartment building. This includes maintenance and repairs, marketing, payroll, utilities, property management, insurance, property taxes, and reserves.

Operating Expense Ratio (OER): A ratio of how efficiently a property is operating by measuring if the rental income will cover the expenses.

Oversubscribed: When a syndication opportunity has gained so much demand from investors, that all of its spots are filled and there is a waiting list.

P

Passive Investing: Hands-off investing where an individual places their money within a real estate syndication managed for them.

Preferred Return (Pref): The minimum agreed-upon return Limited Partners must receive first in a syndication offering before General Partners are paid.

Physical Occupancy Rate: The rate of units with a signed lease (not accounting if the tenants actually pay rent or not).

Prepayment Penalty: A penalty given to lenders if a loan balance is paid off earlier than its agreed-upon timeline.

Private Placement Memorandum (PPM): See definition on Offering Memorandum.

Price Per Unit: The value price of an apartment building, per unit. This is a common metric used when comparing the value and rental income returns of apartment buildings.

Pro forma: The projected income and expenses of an apartment complex.

Property Management Fee: A fee paid to the General Partnership or a third-party professional management company for overseeing the daily operations of an investment property.

Promote (also known as Carried Interest): The bonus paid to General Partners for delivering strong returns to the Limited Partners. It motivates and or rewards Sponsors to exceed the projected returns. The percentage split of profits and equity in a syndication deal that the General Partnership receives after Limited Partners receive their preferred return.

Profit and Loss Statement: A report that lists the income and expenses for an apartment building for a specific period.

R

Ratio Utility Billing System (RUBS): A fancy way of saying that tenants will be billed back for their utility costs.

Refinance: When a new debt service loan (with different terms) is placed on an investment property to replace the previous one.

Rent Roll: A document or spreadsheet that lists the details of every unit in an apartment complex. It usually includes metrics such as the unit numbers, tenant names, square fit, unit mix, market rents, actual rents, security deposits, move-in and move-out dates, and start and end lease dates.

Recourse Loan: Loan that allows the lender to collect from the borrower's personal assets if they default on the loan.

Reserves: Money set aside by Operators to cover repairs, maintenance, renovations, and emergencies.

Rent Premium: The increase in rent applied to a unit after noticeable renovations and upgrades have been made.

Regulation D 506(b): An offering that allows the General Partnership to raise money for a syndication with up to 35 non-accredited investors and an unlimited number of Accredited investors. General Partners cannot advertise the deal publicly.

Regulation D 506 (c): An offering that allows the General Partnership to raise money for a syndication from only Accredited investors. The deal can be advertised publicly.

Rental Comps (Comps): Similar to sales comps, rental comps are used to compare the market rents of similar properties within the same area.

Reversion Cap Rate (Reversion Cap): The estimated exit capitalization rate when the real estate syndication is sold.

Reposition: The business strategy employed by the owner or General Partnership to raise the position of a real estate asset in the market through value-add upgrades/renovations and rebranding.

Rent Control: Regulations and laws passed by a city or state that limits rental rate increases landlords can impose on tenants.

Rent to Own: A creative way to purchase a property by renting it first. The monthly rent that the tenant pays goes toward the agreed-upon purchase price. The tenant is essentially making contributions toward a down payment (typically 10 to 20%) that will be used for purchase.

S

Sophisticated Investor: An investor who is deemed to have enough knowledge and or experience on evaluating the risks and performance metrics of an investment they are interested in.

Syndication: When several investors combine their money together to purchase an investment property.

Sensitivity Analysis (Stress Test): Detailed underwriting simulations conducted on a multifamily apartment, such as changing cap rates, varied interest rates, low rental income, large vacancy, etc., to see how a property would perform and how it would affect projected investor returns.

Split: The percentage split in profits and distributions between the Limited Partners and General Partners in a real estate syndication. A common split would be 70/30, where 70% is paid to the Limited Partners and 30% to the General Partners.

Sales Comparison Approach: Method used to estimate the market value of a property based on recent sales from properties with a similar unit mix, layout, and description within the area.

Subscription Agreement: An agreement between the General Partners and the LLC to sell a certain amount of shares to Limited Partners at a specific agreed-upon price.

Soft Commit: A soft verbal or written commitment from an investor on their intent to invest in a real estate syndication.

Securities and Exchange Commission (SEC): A federal government agency founded in 1934 that enforces security regulations and laws, capital formation, and protects investors' interests and rights.

Sponsor: Another word for General Partner (see above definition on General Partner).

Submarket: A smaller area of a larger market. For example, if the MSA is San Diego, a submarket would be a neighborhood such as downtown, Hillcrest, Mission Hills, or Pacific Beach.

Supplemental Loan: A secondary loan added on top of the senior debt of the capital stack that allows investors to access additional capital cheaper than what it would cost to refinance. You're basically taking on additional debt on top of the original loan balance in order to close the gap on a deal that has an assumable mortgage and yield maintenance fees.

Subletting: The act of a tenant renting out an entire unit or room to another individual not on the lease for a specific period.

T

Tenancy in Common (TIC): A form of co-ownership in which two or more individuals are part-owners in an investment property. Their percentage of ownership interest can differ or be equal.

Trailing Three Months (T-3): The profit and loss statement for an apartment complex for the last 3 months. Great for looking at a property's most recent returns, especially if rents or tenant occupancy levels have recently changed. Recent changes would be hard to catch on the T-12.

Trailing Twelve Months (T-12 or TTM): The profit and loss statement for an apartment complex for the last 12 months. Used to find trends and or inconsistencies in the property's profitability.

Turnover Rate (or move-out rate): The percentage of renters that move out of an apartment community. The number of rental unit move-outs in a year divided by the number of retained rental units that year.

U

Underwriting: Analyzing the financials of an apartment complex to estimate the risks, value, projected returns, and an appropriate offer price.

V

Vacancy Rate: The percentage of units within an apartment community that are vacant.

Value-Add: A business model where Operators increase the income and value of a property through interior and exterior renovations and rebranding.

W

Waterfall: A series of return steps in a syndication structure where, as Limited Partners achieve certain income thresholds, General Partners receive a larger stake in profit from the deal. Waterfall hurdles incentivize General Partners to go above and beyond in the operation and profit a syndication deal produces.

V

Vacancy Loss: The cash flow loss on an apartment complex from vacant units.

Y

Yield Maintenance: A prepayment penalty that allows the lender to earn the same yield of interests payments they were scheduled to receive if the borrower had not repaid the loan off earlier than expected. This provision is to protect lenders from a rapid decrease in interest rates.

If you found value in this book, I would be extremely grateful for your positive review on Amazon.com.

Thank you for your time and support.

SCAN TO LEAVE A REVIEW ON AMAZON

ACKNOWLEDGEMENTS

There are many people that have made a huge impact in my real estate career and in developing this book. Although I may not be able to list everyone and am bound to forget names, I would like to especially thank these individuals:

- Keegan Wetzel: A brother, fellow Supply Corps Officer, Naval Academy graduate, and successful real estate investor. Thank you for opening my eyes and exposing me to the world of multifamily real estate.
- Desiree Doubrox: Thank you for taking a chance on me and allowing me to prove the value I could bring to a team on my first syndication opportunity.
- Jennifer Santoso: Thank you for your continuous honest feedback and advice, and for opening up your network to connect me with anyone you felt could add value to my growth as a real estate investor. I appreciate our sincere friendship and the advice on my first capital raise.
- Cliff Luber: A brother, Supply Corps Officer, and successful real estate investor. Thank you for introducing me to my first real estate mastermind and for all your advice on my first capital raise.
- Ike Ekeh: A brother, friend, and the best co-host a podcaster could ask for. I appreciate our conversations and I look forward to continuing to grow in real estate alongside you.
- Cameron Stewart: A brother, amazing insurance broker, and co-host of the Opportunity Knocks meetup. I couldn't have asked for a more genuine, intelligent friend. I always appreciate you and the many real estate networking events we attend together.

- Mike Chisel: A father, Naval Academy graduate, and mentor. Thank you for supporting me and doing all you could as a broker to ensure I closed my first apartment deal.
- Amy Doll: My biggest cheerleader. Thank you for your mentorship on real estate investing and for looking over the inspection report, appraisal, and every real estate document I received on my first deal.
- Jesse DiLillo: A brother, flipper, and successful real estate investor. Thank you for your support and I cherish our bond and ability to mastermind and grow together as real estate brothers in arms.
- Maverick Garcia: A sister, great friend, and the best interior designer I know. Thank you for being my day one and doing an outstanding job and renovating my units on my first apartment complex.
- Daveed Rangel: A brother and superb real estate agent. Thank you for introducing me to the business club and for teaching me how to dress as a business professional. I'll never forget the time you first took me into the tailor shop.
- Anthony & Alexander Evans: Thank you to my two triplets brothers that, even when they didn't fully understand what I was going through in my real estate business, stood by my side and supported me because they knew that my why was to break the generational curse on our family and open new doors for our mother.
- Lynda Evans: Thank you for your sweet, sincere mentorship and for always doing everything in your power to connect me with the key players in the real estate industry within San Diego.
- Steve Sumpter: A brother and multifamily real estate investor in Los Angeles. Thank you for being a listening ear I could vent and talk to when things got tough and that could truly understand what I was going through.

ABOUT THE AUTHOR

A native of Chicago, Illinois, Dre Evans joined a gang on the South Side of Chicago at twelve. In one terrifying moment, with bullets flying past his head, he had to decide: was his desire to belong and find reputation on the streets worth dying for? Just a few days prior, a man he considered his enemy, spoke to him about the opportunity of a lifetime. After years of violence through fights, drive-by shootings, and other such actions, Andre pursued a better path in life.

What happened next shocked the city of Chicago and made history.

In 2016, Dre graduated from the U.S. Naval Academy at the top of his class with a degree in Engineering and became an MIT Fellow and Truman Scholar.

Dre's journey into real estate started when he bought his first $2 million dollar, 4-unit property in Pacific Beach, San Diego. Today, he owns 98 apartment unit doors, co-hosts the #1 real estate meetup in San Diego called Opportunity Knocks (450+ members), and is the host of the Multifamily by the Slice real estate podcast. He is also an expert on the San Diego rental market and was featured on KUSI News San Diego to talk about the economic outlook of real estate trends, housing, and rent growth within San Diego.

He is an author, motivational speaker, and the Founder and CEO of *That's My Property*, a firm that specializes in purchasing apartment real estate that not only provides investors with lucrative, stable returns to achieve financial freedom—but that provides financial education and outreach to young adults and youth in underserved communities.

He is an experienced Naval Officer. In this role, he has been responsible in leadership roles for hundreds of people in high-stress environments and is experienced in accounting, sales, and the management of over $3.8 million in high-value military assets.

Dre lives in San Diego and enjoys working out, reading, art, movies, traveling, and the beach.

ABOUT THAT'S MY PROPERTY

As Chief Executive Officer, I started *That's My Property* to change the narrative about real estate education and investing in Multifamily Properties. Our mission as a firm is to create generational wealth for everyday people by providing them access to apartment opportunities in stable markets that yield double-digit returns. This frees up investors' time to do more with family, friends, and those they love because they don't have to worry about money. They can also now use their gifts to give back to the world and make it a better place.

That's My Property also dedicates a significant amount of its resources to educating youth about financial literacy and real estate.

The logo is a sticky note with the Chicago skyline in the center and a thumbtack holding the sticky note in place. The sticky note itself is a symbol for writing down the goals you want in life as affirmations that lead to manifestation. The name of the business itself, *That's My Property*, is an ongoing, positive manifestation.

Imagine going up to every property or potential deal and saying to yourself, "That's my property." In this way, the name of my business works double, on the material realm, and the spiritual.

"Writing down your dreams and aspirations is like having a sign that says, 'Open for Business' . . . By writing it down, you declare yourself in the game. Putting it on paper alerts the part of your brain known as the reticular activating system to join you in the play."

– Henriette Anne Klauser

Stay Connected

FOLLOW ME ON SOCIAL MEDIA

@drmultifamily

on all platforms!

MULTIFAMILY by the slice
PODCAST
WITH :
DRE EVANS & IKE EKEH

SPEAKING

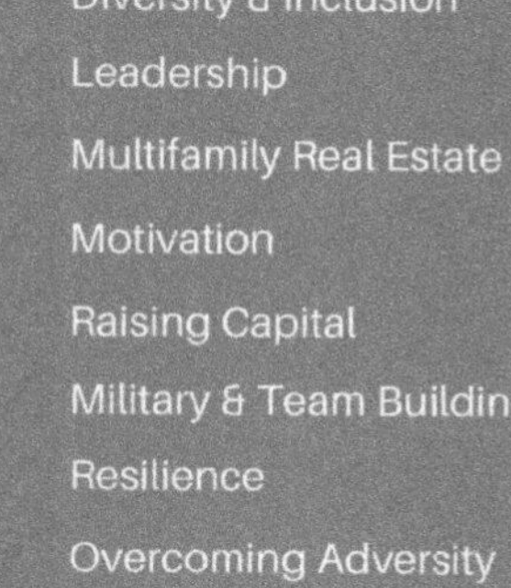
Diversity & Inclusion
Leadership
Multifamily Real Estate
Motivation
Raising Capital
Military & Team Building
Resilience
Overcoming Adversity

Visit website to book
drmultifamily.com

THAT'S MY Investment Goals **Planner**

What are your real estate goals?

How can I add value to help you accompanish them?

What are your total monthly & yearly expenses?

How much passive cash flow would you need to offset your expenses & free up your time?

Book a call with me on my calender & lets make it happen

https://calendly.com/thatsmyproperty

THAT'S MY Passive Income

CERTIFICATE OF COMPLETION

This is to certify that

____

has successfully invested in their first multi-family syndication

____

SIGNATURE

____

DATE

THAT'S MY PURPOSE
Planner

Write down the name of the person who means the most to you in your life

Name: ______________________________

What type of impact do they have on you:

____

____

____

What inspires you?

What type of legacy do you want to leave on the world?

If money was not an issue, what would you pursue or seek to accomplish?

What do you fear most?

What does "greatness" mean to you?

What changes do you need to make to become your best self?

THAT'S MY Investment Goals **Planner**

❶ Goal One:

What excites you most about this goal?

What is the result if you do not acheive this goal?

What has already been the consequences in your life because you have yet to accomplish this goal?

What steps & resources do you need to take to accomplish this goal?

Positive Affirmation: Write out your goal as an affirmation in the past tense (that you already accomplished it)

What is your deadline for accompalishing this goal?

THAT'S MY Investment Goals **Planner**

2 Goal One:

What excites you most about this goal?

What is the result if you do not acheive this goal?

What has already been the consequences in your life because you have yet to accomplish this goal?

What steps & resources do you need to take to accomplish this goal?

Positive Affirmation: Write out your goal as an affirmation in the past tense (that you already accomplished it)

What is your deadline for accompalishing this goal?

THAT'S MY Investment Goals Planner

3 Goal One:

What excites you most about this goal?

What is the result if you do not acheive this goal?

What has already been the consequences in your life because you have yet to accomplish this goal?

What steps & resources do you need to take to accomplish this goal?

Positive Affirmation: Write out your goal as an affirmation in the past tense (that you already accomplished it)

What is your deadline for accompalishing this goal?

THAT'S MY Investment Goals **Planner**

WRITE YOUR ULTIMATE GOAL/CHALLENGE HERE:

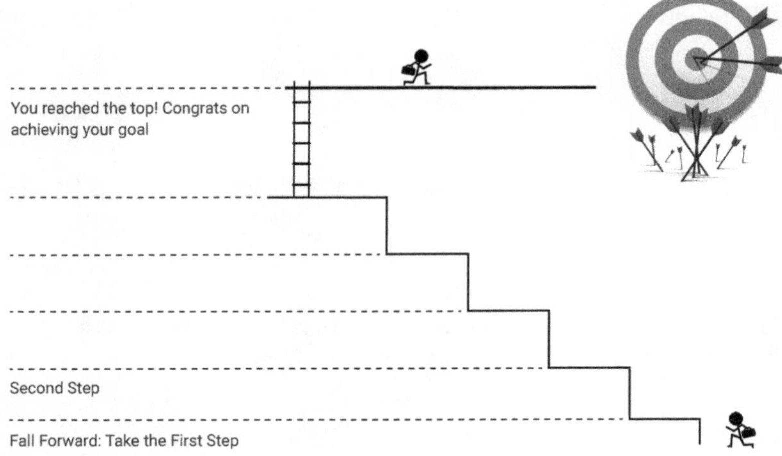

CPSIA information can be obtained
at www.ICGtesting.com
Printed in the USA
JSHW050102250822
29636JS00003B/175

9 781088 057766